Series C
Lent • Easter • Ascension • Pentecost

Study Guide

By Arthur D. Bacon and
Stephen E. Gaulke
Edited by Thomas J. Doyle

SAINT LOUIS

Assistant to the editor: Cindi Crismon

Write to Library for the Blind, 1333 S. Kirkwood Road, St. Louis, MO 63122-7295 to obtain this study in braille or in large print for the visually impared.

Contents

Introduction

About the Series

This course is 1 of 12 in the Church Year series. The Bible studies in this series are tied to the 3-year lectionary. These studies give participants the opportunity to explore the Old Testament lesson (or lesson from the book of Acts during the Easter season), the Epistle lesson, and the Gospel lesson appointed for each Sunday of the church year. Also, optional studies give participants the opportunity to study in-depth the lessons appointed for festival days during the church year that fall on days other than Sunday (e.g., Ascension Day, Reformation, Christmas Day, Christmas Eve, Maundy Thursday, Good Friday, Epiphany).

Book 1 for years A, B, and C in the lectionary series will include 17 studies of the Scripture lessons appointed for the Sundays and festival days in Advent, Christmas, and Epiphany. Book 2 will include 17 studies of the lessons appointed for the Sundays and festival days in Lent and Easter and of lessons appointed for Ascension and Pentecost. Book 3 (15 sessions) and 4 (16 sessions) for years A, B, and C will include studies that focus on the lessons appointed for the Pentecost season.

After a brief review and textual study of the Scripture lessons appointed for a Sunday or festival day, each study is designed to help participants draw conclusions about each of the lessons, compare and contrast the lessons, discover a unifying theme in the lessons (if possible), and apply the theme to their lives. At the end of each study, the Scripture lessons for the next Sunday and/or festival day are assigned for participants to read in preparation for the next study. The leaders guide for each course provides additional textual information on appointed lessons, answers to the questions in the study guide, a suggested process for teaching the study, and devotional or worship activities tied to the theme.

May the Holy Spirit richly bless you as you study God's Word!

Session 1

First Sunday in Lent

Deuteronomy 26:5–10; Romans 10:8b–13; Luke 4:1–13

1 –11

Focus

Theme: *Needs: Needed or Needy*

Law/Gospel Focus

We look to this world for life. "Give me more stuff, more strength, more spectacle," we plead. "World, we need more." The Lord answers, "To you I give My Son!"

Objectives

That by the power of the Holy Spirit working through God's Word we can

1. weigh our needs, and distinguish our godly goals from our evil or self-serving desires;
2. describe how our brother Jesus beat the tempter;
3. call upon our Lord Jesus, admitting our need for a Savior;
4. rejoice in Him whom God has given—the Savior alive, crucified, and risen—to free us from sin and to provide us with abundant life now and into eternity;
5. demonstrate a desire to know God's Word better.

Opening Worship

Pray together:

Leader: Lord, we have desires.

Participants: Our desires have mistreated us.

Leader: Our desires have made us suffer.

Participants: Our desires have put us to hard labor.

Leader: We cry out to You, Lord, the God of our fathers.

Participants: Will You hear our voice?

Leader: Don't we need more of the stuff of this world?

Participants: No, we need more for life than bread alone.

Introduction

1. The boss demands, "Finish your work by Tuesday." The children
   command, "Gimme Cheerios! Gimme movie money! Gimme a
   break!" Well meaning parishioners insist, "(you can) give the
   church one more hour a week." Do you like being a needed person? Why or why not?

   *pulls us off in all directions + distracts
   us from what we want to do*

2. Do you see yourself more as a needed or a needy person? *both*
   Describe being needed or being needy in:

   Your work

   Your play

   Your family

   Your church

   Your God

3. What does God provide to you as both a needed and a needy person?

Inform

Look at the following summaries of the Scripture lessons for the First Sunday in Lent.

Deuteronomy 26:5–10—Moses teaches God's people the "creed" they are to recite when God has brought them to the promised land "flowing with milk and honey." They were asked to recall how God met the needs of their Aramean (Syrian) forefathers, the needs of the generation enslaved in Egypt, and their own needs. Then they will "rejoice in all the good things the LORD your God has given to you and your household" (verse 11).

Romans 10:8b–13—St. Paul rejoices that the Lord has answered our need for salvation by giving His only Son Jesus into death and that by His resurrection Jesus proclaimed victory for us over sin, death, and the power of the devil. Paul says, "confess with your mouth" and "believe in your heart" the resurrected Savior.

Luke 4:1–13—The Spirit leads Jesus from His Baptism out into the wasteland, where for forty days He is tempted by the devil. Three times quoting Scripture, Jesus tells the devil, "I need nothing more than My God."

1. Satan tempts our Savior with the same lies he uses to tempt us. "Tell this stone to become bread." Satan suggests, "If you are God's beloved sons and daughters, why are you so hungry, so needy? Do you believe God loves you? You need more *stuff* from this world!"

    Of all this world's stuff, what makes you feel most needy? What would Satan have us believe about "bread" or "stuff" in this world? Compare Satan's goal with Luther's explanation of the First Commandment, "We should fear, love, and trust in God above all things."

2. "All the kingdoms of the world! All their authority and splendor! If you worship me, it will all be Yours!" Satan insinuates, "If you are God's beloved sons and daughters, why are you the world's weaklings? Do you believe God loves you? You need more *authority and splendor!*"

    How can Satan use your desire to be needed to lead you away from God? What in the world makes you feel weak? Would you rather be the strong master over the world, or ~~serve your~~ strong Master? Why? Give specific examples from your life.

3. "Stand on the highest point of the temple. Throw Yourself down. God promised to command His angels to guard You. They will lift You up in their hands. You will not strike Your foot against a stone." Satan slithers, "If you are God's beloved sons and daughters, why doesn't He wow your world, work wonders? Do you believe God loves you? You need to show us some sign, some *spectacle!*"

   God has worked in you with plain-sounding words, plain-feeling water, plain-tasting bread and wine. What power does God provide to you through His Work in your life? See Acts 2:38; Matthew 26:28; 2 Timothy 3:15. How does this power help you?

4. Satan tempts our Savior with one truth he never could apply to us. Three times he sneers, "If You are the Son of God ... Prove it! Are You really God's Son, or just some second Adam? Prove it! Fight like a God, not like a man!" But what if Jesus does beat the devil by His godly powers, rather than as our brother? Then we lose! Why? See Hebrews 2: 17–18 and Hebrews 4:15–16.

Connect

Our needs and desires of the flesh leave us hungry and despairing. But God fills us with His gifts, gladly. According to Moses' creed, what were the outstanding needs of God's people? What did God do in answer to each generations' own needs? According to the Apostles' and Nicene creeds, how has God answered the same kinds of outstanding needs for His people today?

1. Deuteronomy 26:5. The patriarch Jacob, whom God renamed Israel, was the nation's founding father.
   a. Father Jacob needed …

   b. God gave him …

   c. God gives us …

2. Deuteronomy 26:6–8.
   a. Israel's children once enslaved in Egypt needed …

   b. God gave them …

   c. God gives us … *everything we have*

3. Deuteronomy 26:9.
   a. Israel's children, now given the promised Palestine, needed …

   b. God gave them …

   c. God gives us …

4. Jesus' life of victory against temptation substitutes for our many defeats. Jesus slashed Satan with nothing but the one invincible weapon God would put in the hands of all Jesus' brothers and sisters. With what sword can we Christians now combat the devil, as did Christ? Where do we find that sword according to Romans 10:8–9?

5. The Word of God, in one word, is *Jesus!* Paul rejoices, "Everyone who calls on the name of the Lord will be saved" (Romans 10:13). The name of our Lord, "Jesus," means what? See Matthew 1:21. What does His name mean to you, with your unique needs?

Vision

During This Week

1. Find one Bible passage that clearly speaks to you about your need to know God's Word. Read this to yourself when you rise and when you return to bed. In how many days will you have memorized the words?

2. When you feel tempted, rejoice that your brother Jesus beat the tempter. When the devil reminds you of your past, remind him of his future.

3. Notice how Moses' creed climaxed with the believer's deed. "Place the basket" of the promised land's firstfruits before Him who promised, and "bow down" worshiping Him (Deuteronomy 26:10).

    What is your Christian creed? Has God met your needs? "He who did not spare His own Son, but gave Him up for us all—how will He not also, along with Him, graciously give us all things?" (Romans 8:32). How will you, this week, live your creed in deed?

Closing Worship

Pray together:

Leader: Lord, we have desires.

Participants: Our desires have mistreated us.

Leader: Our desires have made us suffer.

Participants: Our desires have put us to hard labor.

Leader: We cry out to You, Lord, the God of our fathers.

Participants: Will You hear our voice?

Leader: We do not need more stuff, more splendor, more spectacle.

Participants: Lord, we need You!

Leader: We need to admit with our mouths,

Participants: Jesus is Lord!

Leader: We need to believe in our hearts,

Participants: God raised Him from the dead!

Leader: You will be saved.

Participants: Everyone who calls on the name
                    of the Lord will be saved.
Leader: Lord, You have heard our voice!
Participants: You have seen our misery, toil, and oppression.
Leader: With Your mighty hands,
Participants: Hands pierced by nails!
Leader: With Your out-stretched arms,
Participants: Arms stretched out on the cross!
Leader: You have freed us from our greatest needs!
Participants: We bow down and worship You, O Lord Jesus, our
                    resurrected God!

Scripture Lessons for Next Sunday

Read Jeremiah 26:8–15; Philippians 3:17–4:1; and Luke 13:31–35
in preparation for the next session.

Session 2

Second Sunday in Lent

Jeremiah 26:8–15; Philippians 3:17–4:1; Luke 13:31–35

Focus

Theme: *The Master Plan*

Law/Gospel Focus

We fail to mold our life's plan to the Master's plan. Jesus not only executed our rescue, but plans our life to further His grand design.

Objectives

By the power of the Holy Spirit working through God's Word we will
1. review our life's plan … and past surprises;
2. rejoice at God's plan, through which we receive life everlasting;
3. reconsider how Christ's cross molds our life's plan.

Opening Worship

Pray together:

Leader: "On the third day I will reach My goal," promised Jesus.

Participants: We believe that on the third day He rose from the dead.

Leader: Jesus gathered us together, safe under His wing.

Participants: He has gathered us to His holy Christian church, the communion of saints.

Leader: Jesus will transform our lowly bodies to be like His glorious body.

Participants: He will lead us to life everlasting.

All: Blessed is Jesus! Blessed is He who comes in the name of the Lord!

Introduction

Do you have a "five year plan"? Describe yourself in five years.

1. What will you have accomplished with your work?

   No - Day by Day - Month by Month - Vacation plan

2. With what leisure activities will you be involved?

   Dine out - KC.R

3. Describe your family.

   Dave & myself involved in all KC activities
   or Caring for others - helping others - Doing for others

4. How does your faith shape your plans?

   helping others thinking of others praying for others

5. How have you seen God bless your plans during the past five years? *yes - Many times*

6. What good has God worked in your life through unplanned events? *Made us available to others*

=============== **Inform** ===============

Look at the following summaries of the Scripture lessons for the Second Sunday in Lent.

Jeremiah 26:8–15—Judah's priests and phony prophets, excited at the prospect of their new king Jehoiakim (609 B.C.), had big plans. With the help of Egypt, they would free God's tiny province from commander Nebuchadnezzar's new Babylonian Empire. But the Lord sends Jeremiah to tell His plan to the people of Judah. As sure as the Lord once abandoned the town of His holy Tabernacle, Shiloh, now He will abandon the city of His holy temple, Jerusalem.

Judah's supreme court gathers at the gate of God's temple. Jeremiah, if guilty of treason and blasphemy, should be sentenced to death. But Jeremiah said, "The LORD sent me. Now reform your ways and your actions and obey the LORD your God. Then the LORD will relent and not bring the disaster He has pronounced against you."

Philippians 3:17–4:1—"Join with others in following my example," says St. Paul. "Live according to the pattern we gave you." People, sad to say, make their own plans. They "live as enemies of the cross of Christ…. But our citizenship is in heaven." From there comes our Savior. He plans to resurrect us in glorious bodies. So "stand firm in the Lord, dear friends!"

Luke 13:31–35—Some Pharisees warn Jesus of a plot against His life, "Herod wants to kill You." They urge Him to flee. Jesus refuses to flee. "And on the third day I will reach my goal." Humanity's most malicious conspiracy will fulfill God's grand design, prophesies Jesus, "for surely no prophet can die outside Jerusalem!"

Still, Jesus' heart breaks over the wickedness of God's people. "O Jerusalem, Jerusalem…. Look, your house is left to you desolate." Still, Jesus' heart rejoices over the wonder of God's plan. At last even Jerusalem must say, "Blessed is He who comes in the name of the Lord."

1. Jesus prophesies, "Look, your house is left to you desolate." When did that happen?

   Some Bible students point to the Roman legion's destruction of Jerusalem's temple (God's house) and the leveling of their whole city home in A.D. 70.

   Others recall that all Jewish hopes for the revival of the Davidic royal "house" died with that final Zealots' revolt against Rome.

   "All the people seized Jeremiah. 'Why do you prophesy in the LORD's name that this house will be like Shiloh and this city will be desolate and deserted?'" (Jeremiah 26:9).

   Both in Jesus' day and Jeremiah's, the Lord allowed the armies of unbelievers to smash the plots of Israel's pious patriots. Why? Clue: Were the pious patriots "doing this for God," or were they trusting God to do for them?

2. Can you remember once when your plans, or even your desire to

14

"do this for God," did not happen? How did you feel about that failure then? Can you now see what good God gave to you out of that disappointment?

yes - many thing happen - not in our plan.

3. God had a plan to rescue His people. Jerusalem's temple "house" and David's royal "house" were but the shadows of His grand design.

    Already the angel Gabriel had told the virgin mother Mary, "The Lord God will give Him the throne of His father David, and He will reign over the house of Jacob forever" (Luke 1:32–33).

    How does Jesus first reveal God's plan in John 2:18–22? Did those who plotted Jesus' death "get it"? Read Matthew 26:59–66 and Matthew 27:38–43.

4. Jesus prophesied, "Look, your house is left to you desolate" (Luke 13:35). The Lord did leave His temple "house," the "house" of David's royal descendant, desolate! The Crucified shouts, "My God, My God, why have You forsaken Me?" (Matthew 27:46).

    Forsaken, why? "Because You carry the sins of the world, Your Father actually abandons You, crucified to the very pain of hell." What good has God planned for you by this desolation, this desertion, the literal damnation of His Son? How do you respond to God's plan?

5. Jesus prophecies, "I tell you, you (Jerusalem) will not see Me again until you say, 'Blessed is He who comes in the name of the Lord!'" When did that happen?

Some Bible students point to Jerusalem's welcome on Palm Sunday. "Hosanna to the Son of David!" (Matthew 21:9). "Blessed is the King who comes in the name of the Lord!" (Luke 19:38).

Others point to the "new Jerusalem," the millions of Jew and Gentile converts who "see" the risen Jesus by faith and joyfully say, "Blessed is He!"

Still others point to the Last Day. "At the name of Jesus every knee should bow ... and every tongue confess that Jesus Christ is Lord" (Philippians 2:10–11).

How might each of these answers be correct?

6. The Son of David has fulfilled the Lord's plan! When do you bless Him who came to your rescue in the name of the Lord? Jesus does not leave you desolate, but comes to you today. How?

══ **Connect** ══

1. "On the third day I will reach my goal," promised Jesus (Luke 13:32). "The third day He rose again from the dead," we confess in the Apostles' Creed. Jesus still longs to gather God's children together, as a hen gathers her chicks under her wings (Luke 13:34). The risen Christ has gathered us to "the holy Christian church, the communion of saints."

   Is God's goal accomplished? See Philippians 3:18–20. How do you and your church fit into the Master's plan?

2. Sheltered under mother hen's outstretched wings, the chicks are safe from the eagles. Sheltered under Jesus' arms, once stretched out on the cross, we are safe from sin, death, and Satan. He shields us until "the resurrection of the body, and the life everlasting."

St. Paul speaks of that "resurrection" and "life" in Philippians 3:20–21. Does Paul describe you as a native of this world, hoping to emigrate to heaven? Or are you an alien visiting earth, holding the passport from your true Fatherland? What difference does that make in your life's plan?

3. "Take up your cross and follow me," invites our Savior (Mark 8:34). St. Paul took this deathstyle for His lifestyle. "Follow my example," says he, "and take note of those who live according to the pattern we gave you" (Philippians 3:17). From whose lifestyle have you learned the faith? What example would you like loved ones to see in you?

4. "On the third day I will reach my goal," promised Jesus (Luke 13:32). Christ's death ends in resurrection. So does yours. You will reach your goal! According to Philippians 3:21, how will your resurrected body be different from your dying body?

5. Two vivid emotions color today's Scripture readings. One is mournful grieving. The other is joyful longing. For what did Jesus long? What moved Him to grief? For what does Paul long? Do you weep over this world's rejection of the Crucified? How does your rejoicing testify to Jesus' resurrection? *We can believe his promises*

His Father in heaven

People Not believing

Vision

During This Week

1. Notice when you mourn and when you rejoice. Ask yourself, "Is my grief, my longing, stirred by godly goals? How can my feelings better reflect my faith?"
2. Stretching out your arms like the mother hen's wings, hug your loved ones. Tell them, "Jesus is going to resurrect me with stronger arms. I'll give tighter hugs in His soon to come world!"
3. In your daily devotions, rejoice that God has not left your home desolate. Read Jesus' Word. Thank Him for His sacramental love. Ask Him to use you in His Master plan!

Closing Worship

Pray together:

Leader: Lord, give us tears,

Participants: For many live as enemies of the cross of Christ.

Leader: Lord, gives us grins,

Participants: For our citizenship is in heaven.

Leader: Lord, focus our eyes on Your plan, that we may ever follow You.

Participants: Let others see Your cross, Your pattern in our life, that they too may ever trust and follow You.

All: Blessed is Jesus! He comes in the name of the Lord.

Scripture Lessons for Next Sunday

Read Exodus 3:1–8a, 10–15; 1 Corinthians 10:1–13; and Luke 13:1–9 in preparation for the next session.

Session 3

Third Sunday in Lent

Exodus 3:1–8a, 10–15; 1 Corinthians 10:1–13; Luke 13:1–9

Isa 55:1-9 (handwritten)
Ro 63 1-8 (handwritten)

Focus

Theme: *Excuse Me*

Law/Gospel Focus

"To err is human." We sinfully make excuses for our failure to live our faith fruitfully. But God does not dismiss our self-excusing as trivial. "To forgive is divine." He did the hard work, not simply to excuse our sins, but to forgive and forget them fully.

Objectives

By the power of the Holy Spirit working through God's Word we will

1. describe God's unwillingness to simply dismiss our sinful excuses; *be forgiven (handwritten)*
2. realize that because God could not simply excuse sin, He laid His anger and wrath upon His Son on the cross to win forgiveness for us;
3. desire Christ's forgiveness and the strengthening for Christ like living He provides in His sacraments;
4. share Christ's love, forgiving those who have sinned against us and proclaiming Christ's forgiveness.

Opening Worship

Pray together:

Leader: Warn us, Lord, by those who wandered away from You.

Participants: All Israel You delivered from the hands of the Egyptians.

Leader: They all ate Your spiritual food.

Participants: They all drank Your spiritual drink.
Leader: Still, they set their hearts on evil things.
Participants: And You were not pleased with them.
Leader: Unless we turn from sin, we too will perish!
Participants: Unless we turn toward You, Lord, we all will perish!
Leader: By Your Word and sacraments, feed our faith.
Participants: By Your Word and sacraments, make us fruitful.
All: In the Name of the Father, Son, and Holy Spirit. Amen.

Introduction

My wife and I have our excuses. Sometimes she senses some teeny, tiny, totally inaudible bubble in her throat. "Excuse me," she mutters, absentmindedly. I wonder aloud, "For what?"

Sometimes I let slip some larger, louder burp. Sarcastically, I spout, "Excuuuuse me." She wonders, "Must you belch so boorishly?"

In so many ways we say "Excuse me." Often, without admitting fault at all: "Excuse me. Do you know the way to the grocery store?" As heartfelt apology: "I am so sorry that I hurt you. Could you ever excuse me?" Or to make a molehill of the mountain: "Excuse me. I was driving only nine miles over the speed limit?!" Maybe to escape our angry accuser: "Are you finished yet? May I be excused now?" Even in self-defense: "Excuse me! How was I to know you put the plug in the bathtub drain?"

1. When last did you say, "Excuse me"? Why?

2. When have you said "Excuse me" to God? Why?

Inform

Read the following summaries of the Scripture lessons for the Third Sunday in Lent.

Exodus 3:1–8a, 10–15—"Excuse me?" Moses' eyes open wide. "You want me?" Forty years before, when he had lived as the Pharaoh's son, Moses fancied himself as the Hebrews' rescuer. Then he struck one slave driver dead. Now, he is an eighty-year-old fugitive. Should he go back to free the ungrateful slaves?

Moses makes excuses. "Who am I, that I should go to Pharaoh and bring the Israelites out of Egypt?" And, "Suppose they ask me, 'What is God's name?'" Even after the Lord's assurances in today's text, Moses makes more excuses. "What if they do not believe me?" (Exodus 4:1). Again, "I am slow of speech and tongue" (4:10). Finally, "O Lord, please send someone else to do it" (4:13). "Excuse me!"

But the Lord will not excuse Egypt. "I have indeed seen the misery of my people ... I have come down to rescue them ... I am sending you."

1 Corinthians 10:1–13—"Excuse me!" Paul interrupts the Corinthian Christians' day dreams. "If you think you are standing firm, be careful that you don't fall!"

The faithless use of God's Sacrament will not spare us from God's displeasure. Once when all Israel followed their Lord, who was present in the pillar of cloud, "they were all baptized." They were "baptized" into Moses as he led them to freedom from Egypt's slavery through the Red Sea. All Israel "ate the same spiritual food and drank the same spiritual drink." They daily ate heaven's manna, and as they wandered through the wilderness wasteland, God gave them water from a supernatural rock. "They drank from the spiritual rock that accompanied them, and that rock was Christ."

Still, of that whole generation only Caleb and Joshua entered the promised land. They all died in the desert. Why? Idolatry. Sexual immorality. Testing the Lord. Grumbling. These things stand written "as examples to keep us from setting our hearts on evil things as they did."

Take to heart God's Word and sacraments, and so live faithfully. Stand tall! God will rescue you from all temptation. No excuses.

Luke 13:1–9—"Excuse ye!" proclaims Jesus. "Do you think these so suffered because they were worse sinners, more guilty, than others?" Neither the Galileans, slaughtered by Governor Pilate when they brought their sacrifices to God's temple, nor the Jerusalemites crushed when the Siloam tower fell, give you excuse. "Unless you repent, you too will all perish."

Jesus tells the parable of the fruitless fig tree. The fact that the tree still stands does not forever excuse its barren limbs. The vineyard owner has excused the tree, but has given it one more year to respond to the keeper's care. Excuses end!

1. The drunk driver crashed into Jill's car. "Lord! What did she do to deserve this?" her neighbor puzzled.

   Jack's house crumpled under the tornado. His insurer called this "an act of God."

   Can we read our neighbor's troubles as God's public notice of displeasure with that person's sins? According to Luke 13:1–5, why not? *No - but !*

   unless we repent we will all perish

2. "Unless you repent, you too will all perish." Jesus' word "perish" fully means "be destroyed, lost, damned." "Most merciful God.... We justly deserve your present and eternal punishment. (Divine Service II, *LW*, p. 158). Which sounds more harsh to you: the confession of sins from our worship service or Jesus' sentence? Why?
   Jesus was God Son.
   we also are God children!

   Yet God does have mercy and does not punish sinners! Why?
   He forgives + forgets

3. "Unless you repent ..." warns Jesus. "Repent" comes from the Hebrew prophets' word, "Turn around!" Jesus would have us mournfully turn away from what, and joyfully turn toward whom? In what two parts of the worship service do we repent?
   Turn away from Sin & turn toward God

4. The first of Martin Luther's Ninety-five Theses reads, "When our

22

Lord and Master Jesus Christ said, 'Repent,' He willed the entire life of believers to be one of repentance" (Luther's Works, Volume 31, page 25). When the worship service is finished, how do you live repentance all week long?

Connect

1. Mack gets his pay raise. "Somebody up there likes me," he points.
   Mary hits the jackpot. "Lord, how You smile on me," she trumpets her triumph.
   Can you read your continued strong standing as God's plain guarantee of good pleasure with you? According to Luke 13:6–9, why not?

   daily repentance + asking for forgiveness

2. Perhaps we, like the fruitless fig tree, have been excused once more. But the parable does tell how the vineyard keeper plans to care for us. What does Jesus do today to "dig around" and "fertilize" your faith? With what garden tools has he promised to work in your life? *to encourage us to produce.*

3. Did not God work in old Israel sacramentally? They were "all baptized ... They all ate the same spiritual food and drank the same spiritual drink ... Nevertheless, God was not pleased with most of them" (1 Corinthians 10:2–5). Why not? Their idolatry, sexual immorality, testing the Lord, and grumbling all truly told who they trusted as their god. In whom did they trust? *themselves + the world around them*

4. Did Israel's baptism, and their spiritual food and drink, fail them? Or did they fail these gifts? Explain.

No – they failed

5. Baptism "works forgiveness of sins, rescues from death and the devil, and gives eternal salvation to all who believe this, as the words and promises of God declare," says Luther's Small Catechism. But how can water do such great things? "Certainly not just water, but the word of God in and with the water does these things, along with the faith which trusts the word of God." Or, how can bodily eating and drinking do such great things? "Certainly not just eating and drinking do these things, but the words written here: 'Given and shed for you for the forgiveness of sins.'... Whoever believes these words has exactly what they say: 'forgiveness of sins.' "

I get the benefit of what God's Word clearly promises in His sacraments only if I *believe + ask for forgiveness*

All the sins of the world the Lord has forgiven. But God would not excuse Israel's continued failure of *disobedience*

The Lord has loaded forgiveness in His sacraments. But Israel had used His sacraments fruitlessly, without *prayer.*

"These things happened to them as examples and were written down as warnings for us" (1 Corinthians 10:11). *of God wrath if we do not obey + ask for forgiveness*

6. We have no excuse. "God is faithful" (1 Corinthians 10:13). But Israel's faithlessness showed itself in her fruitlessness. Israel fell for sin's temptations.

"If you think you are standing firm, be careful that you don't fall!" (1 Corinthians 10:12). Can Christ's sacraments help you stand, living your faith in real life? How? Picture Baptism's power according to Romans 6:1–4. Report the Supper's benefit according to 1 Corinthians 11:26.

24

7. Does God judge "the devil made me do it" a worthy excuse? What does God promise you in 1 Corinthians 10:13?

No

He will not test you beyond your strength but will provide a way out — forgiveness —

How does your Baptism and Jesus' Feast "provide a way out so that you can stand up under temptation"?

We were renewed as God's child — we need to ask for daily forgiveness

Vision

During This Week

1. Thank God every day for your Holy Baptism.
2. God turned Moses around. God sent him back to Egypt brandishing God's Word to free the slaves.
   You hold the invincible sword of Christ's forgiveness, His weapon to free sin's slaves. Ask the Lord, "To whom would You send me?" Then go!
3. Moses had his excuses. Suppose he took a 3″ × 5″ note card and wrote down his excuses. On the flip side, he could write down God's answers!
   We have our excuses. Suppose you wrote down yours. Starting with Exodus 3:1–15, find some promises in God's Word that speak to your excuses. Write them down on the card's other side. Carry God's promises in your purse or wallet this week.

Closing Worship

Pray together:

Leader: Lead us, Lord, by Christ.

Participants: You join all Christians to Jesus through Holy Baptism.

Leader: We all eat Your spiritual food, the body of our risen Savior.

Participants: We all drink Your spiritual drink, the blood of Christ,

25

the living Rock.

Leader: Set our hearts on Your good sacraments,

Participants: That we may be pleasing to You.

Leader: Unless we turn from sin, we too will perish!

Participants: Unless we turn towards You, Lord, we will all perish!

Leader: By Your Word and sacraments, feed our faith.

Participants: By Your Word and sacraments, make us fruitful.

All: In the Name of the Father, Son, and Holy Spirit. Amen.

Scripture Lessons for Next Sunday

Read Isaiah 12:1–6; 1 Corinthians 1:18–31; and Luke 15:1–3, 11–32 in preparation for the next session.

Session 4

Fourth Sunday in Lent

Isaiah 12:1–6; 1 Corinthians 1:18–31; Luke 15:1–3, 11–32

Focus

Theme: *But Now I'm Found*

Law/Gospel Focus

Although I put myself, my satisfaction, and my desire above everything else, my heavenly Father restored me to His family, even at the cost of His one and only Son.

Objectives

By the power of the Holy Spirit working through God's Word we will

1. recognize the separation from God resulting from our self-wasting and self-righteousness;
2. rejoice that our strong and wise Father restored our relationship to Him through His only Son's death;
3. seek to reconcile differences we have with our brothers and sisters.

Opening Worship

Sing or pray together stanzas 1 and 3 of "Amazing Grace" (*LW* 509).

Amazing grace! How sweet the sound
That saved a wretch like me!
I once was lost but now am found,
Was blind but now I see!

Through many dangers, toils, and snares
I have already come;
His grace has brought me safe so far,
His grace will see me home.

Introduction

1. What would you do or say if your son said, "Drop dead, Dad. No, don't make me wait that long. Just give me my hunk of the inheritance today, and I'm out of here"? *then go.*

2. What would you do and/or say if after squandering his inheritance the same boy returned home penniless? *Take him back*

3. How would you react to your brother's return if you were an older sibling who had stood beside and had been obedient to your father? *with Jelousy*

4. What matters most to you in your family and friendships? Rank these four in order of importance beginning with 1 denoting *the most important*:
   _____ Fair rewards
   _____ Forgiveness
   _____ Right behavior
   _____ Not fighting

5. Explain the reason for your ranking.

Inform

Look at the following summaries of the Scripture lessons for the Fourth Sunday in Lent.

Isaiah 12:1–6—Isaiah's twin songs praise and give thanks to Israel's Lord. Yes, Israel has been God's prodigal son, worthy only of the Father's anger. Still, praise! For "the LORD, the LORD, is my strength and my song; He has become my salvation." Give thanks! For doing so you "make known among the nations what He has done."

1 Corinthians 1:18–31—God's wisdom, God's strength, and God's work is not understood or appreciated by the world in which we live. "We preach Christ crucified." God works through the lips of sinners. God works by His Word of Jesus crucified (weakness) and Jesus resurrected (foolishness).

God works for our redemption. "Think of what you were when you were called … God chose the foolish … God chose the weak …It is because of Him that you are in Christ Jesus."

God's children cannot boast in self-righteousness. Unlike the prodigal's big brother, they boast not in their slavish obedience, nor moan about the Father's "weak" and "foolish" forgiveness. Those made holy by Jesus' forgiveness rejoice to "boast in the Lord."

Luke 15:1–3, 11–32—Jesus stands accused by the Pharisees and teachers of Moses' law. "This man welcomes sinners," and is so comfortably intimate with them that He even "eats with them." Jesus answers with the parables of the lost sheep, the lost coin, and then, the lost son.

A man has two sons. The younger one grasps his share of the Father's estate and strays. He proves himself the prodigal. Having squandered his wealth in wild living, he hits bottom in the pig pen. Hardly kosher! At last remembering his father's kindness, he rehearses his homecoming confession of sin. He would be thrilled to be one of his father's hired hands. But his father won't hear of it. As he runs to hug his son, kiss him, and offer him a robe, ring, sandals, and a high feast, the father fully forgives and restores the boy. "He was lost and is found."

That's why Jesus welcomes and feasts with known sinners!

The elder son has no clue how far his heart has wandered from his father. He has made himself miserable, the obedient slave. His father leaves the feast to find this son, too. He would set the boy free to rejoice in the riches he has always had.

Jesus' hearers must write the end of the story. Will this elder lost son let himself be found? Will the Pharisees come home to receive their Father's "weak" and "foolish" forgiveness? Will we, who have wandered, come home to receive our Father's forgiveness?

1. Find the seed of the younger son's troubles in his first demand (verse 12). Do you see yourself in this son? How so?

2. What warning (Law) does the prodigal's story hold for you? What comfort (Gospel) does this son's story promise you? Compare Ephesians 2:4–5.

Saved by grace

3. "Give me," demanded the younger son. Find the seed of the elder son's troubles in his final accusation (verse 29). Do you see yourself in this son? How so?

Worked like a slave & did not get any benefits

4. What warning (Law) does the elder son's story hold for you? What comfort (Gospel) does this son's story promise you? Compare Romans 10:12b.

5. "The foolishness of God is wiser than man's wisdom, and the weakness of God is stronger than man's strength," preaches Paul in 1 Corinthians 1:25. Jesus' parable pictures this. How does the father look foolish and weak? How does this show our heavenly Father's wisdom and strength?

Connect

1. Roleplay the father and younger son's reunion. Then act out the father and elder son's showdown. Put emotion into the words Jesus gives His characters. Make up responses for the two sons.

2. The father offers his hands in love to the found son. The robe that replaces his rags tells of the lost son's restored status. The ring,

perhaps used to seal official documents, gives his father's authority. The sandals, since slaves often go barefoot, show his sonship. By the feast, for which the father sacrifices the one fattened calf, his very best, the father "welcomes" the sinner son "and eats with him." Would his father's hug and kiss matter to the son? Why?

3. Our heavenly Father offers His hand in love to you. How? See Galatians 3:26–27 and Luke 22:19–20. Do these, like our Father's verbal promise, matter to you? Why?

4. Jesus' story has this happy ending. The prodigal son has been welcomed home! What might this son now say to his father? See Isaiah 12:1–3. Does Isaiah's song fit your mouth? Why?

5. Also with his elder son, the father may yet live happily ever after. After all his pleading with and pledging himself to this son, what would the father love to hear this son say? See Isaiah 12:4–6. Would these words come from your lips? Why?

6. Millions still wonder. "Jesus, You tell one wonderful story. But why ever should God act so foolishly as to forgive sinners, or so weakly as to reach out towards self-righteous 'slaves'?" Jesus does not just talk a good story. According to 1 Corinthians 1:23–24, what is the wisdom and power of God? How do you demonstrate the wisdom and power of God in your life?

Vision

During This Week

1. This week in your personal prayers, praise your heavenly Father. He welcomes you into His eternal home! Give thanks. Already now He feasts with you at your worship home!
2. Whom do you know like the prodigal son, who is self-wasted and searching for home? How can you reflect your Father's welcoming love towards him or her?

3. Whom do you know like the elder son, who is self-righteous and bitter about home? How can you mirror your Father's pleading love toward that one?

Closing Worship

Pray together:

Leader: "Let's have a feast and celebrate," our Father rejoices.

Participants: This is the feast of victory for our God!

Leader: Sings He, "For this Son of Mine was dead and is alive again."

Participants: Worthy is Christ, the Lamb who was slain, whose blood set us free to be people of God.

Leader: "We preach Christ crucified," rejoices St. Paul. "Christ the power of God. Christ the wisdom of God."

Participants: Power, riches, wisdom, and strength, and honor, blessing, and glory are His!

Leader: "Give thanks to the Lord," sings Isaiah. "Make known among the nations what He has done."

Participants: Thank the Lord and sing His praise. Tell everyone what He has done!

All: We once were lost but now are found. This we shall ever celebrate!

Scripture Lessons for Next Sunday

Read Isaiah 43:16–21; Philippians 3:8–14; and Luke 20:9–19 in preparation for the next session.

Session 5

Fifth Sunday in Lent

Isaiah 43:16–21; Philippians 3:8–14; Luke 20:9–19

Theme: *Damned if You Do ... Delivered if You Don't*

Law/Gospel Focus

"Damned if you do," Jesus warns those who would reject Him. "Delivered if you don't," rejoice all who receive Him. The Holy Son of the living God freely gives His righteousness and the blessings and promise of His resurrection to all who trust in Him.

Objectives

By the power of the Holy Spirit working through God's Word we will

1. respond to Jesus' warning that those who reject God's Son determine their fate—damnation;
2. rejoice at Jesus' promise to forgive our former sinful rubbish and to take hold of us today, granting us His righteousness through faith, and to call us heavenward to live with Him when we die;
3. resolve to reflect Jesus' love as we love and forgive others.

Opening Worship

Pray together:

Leader: This is what the Lord says—He who made a way through the Red Sea,

Participants: who opened our dry path through the mighty waters,

Leader: who drew out Egypt's chariots and horses,

Participants: the army and reinforcements together,

> Leader: and they lay there, never to rise again,
> Participants: our enemies extinguished, snuffed out like a wick.
> Leader: The Lord says, "Forget the former things; do not dwell on the past."
> Participants: "See, I am doing a new thing!"

Introduction

Last week's parable highlighted the prodigal son. Jesus showed our heavenly Father's amazing grace. The father permits His heart to be broken by his runaway boy. Still, he gladly welcomes home the wasted one who returns.

But is it always loving to let the one you love abuse your love? When does God's love necessitate confronting those who persist in self-love?

Inform

Look at the following summaries of the Scripture lessons for the Fifth Sunday in Lent.

Isaiah 43:16–21—Isaiah recalls the very heart of Israel's faith. Seven hundred years before, the Lord had rescued Moses' people at the Red Sea. But now, says the Lord, "Forget the former things … See, I am doing a new thing!"

In the old days, the Lord led Israel safely through the desert wasteland to the promised land. Isaiah prophesied that fruitless, faithless Israel would be delivered to new bondage in Babylon. Even so, the Lord now promises, the repentant remnant He will bring home again to Palestine.

Why is the Lord again and again so forgiving? He forgives so that "the people I formed for Myself … may proclaim My praise."

Philippians 3:8–14—"Forgetting what is behind," St. Paul "considers everything a loss." All his past pleasure, profit, power, and pride he now considers "rubbish."

35

"Straining toward what is ahead," St. Paul would "gain Christ" and "the righteousness that comes from God and is by faith." Even by his present sufferings and death Paul wants "to know Christ and the power of His resurrection."

"I press on to take hold of that for which Christ Jesus took hold of me." Paul's faith looks not backward but forward. "I press on toward the goal to win the prize for which God has called me heavenward in Christ Jesus."

Luke 20:9–19—Jesus speaks this parable against the teachers of Moses' holy Law and the chief priests of David's holy temple. When they have killed the Lord's holy Son, "What then will the owner of the vineyard do to them? He will come and kill those tenants and give the vineyard to others."

Why such an awful end? The villains look back, determined to hold this privileged property even with the son's blood on their hands. They do not look forward, delighted in the prospect of future friendship with the generous Lord who has leased them His fruitful vineyard.

God's triumphant capstone must crush those who obstinately oppose Him.

1. Identify the players in Jesus' parable.
   Who is the owner who planted the vineyard?

   What is that vineyard?

   Who are the tenants of the owner who owe him a share of his vineyard's crop?

   What is the harvest fruit the tenant owed to the owner?

   Who are the servants whom the owner sends: the one beaten by the tenants, another treated shamefully, a third wounded and thrown out, all of whom returned empty-handed?

   Who is the owner's son, "my son, whom I love"?

Who are the others to whom at last the owner gives his vineyard?

2. Wild! Why would the tenant farmers beat the owner's servants, and send them back without his share of his crop? Would you abuse the servants your Lord sends to you and send them away empty-handed?

3. "If we let Him go on like this, everyone will believe in Him, and then the Romans will come and take away both our place and our nation" (John 11:48). Israel's religious leaders put their promised property and privileges first.

   "I have lost all things. I consider them rubbish so that I may gain Christ." Why would St. Paul gladly give up what Israel's religious leaders would not? What do you treasure?

4. Weird! Why would this landlord send, not swift justice, but still more servants to these fruitless farmers? How has your Owner, God Himself, shown patience to you?

5. Wonderful! What father, really, would figure so foolishly? "What shall I do? I will send my son, whom I love; perhaps they will respect him." What love has the heavenly Father shown towards you? How is God's love foolish, unreal by this world's standards?

6. Crazy love gets clobbered by crazy hatred! Perhaps they figured his father was dead? "This is the heir," conspired the tenants. Per-

haps they would claim squatters' rights to the ownerless property. "Let's kill him, and the inheritance will be ours." Have you ever acted as if God were dead? What role did your crazy hatred play in the killing of Christ?

Connect

1. When he sends his son, the father shows the length of his love (Gospel). The father so longs to restore the relationship between his tenants and himself that he gives his one, beloved son!

   At the same time, in sending his son, the father shows the outer limit of his tolerance (Law).

   Does the parable suggest that those damned, in the end, are damned due to their wicked deeds? Or damned for their rejection of the Father's one, beloved Son? Note how Jesus warns those who plot His murder in Luke 20:17–18.

2. Are we, in the end, delivered due to our good deeds? Or are we delivered solely through the merits of the Father's one, beloved Son? Note how Paul invites us to grasp Jesus' life in Philippians 3:9.

3. What's the difference between "everyone who falls on that stone" and "he on whom it falls"? Some people actively reject Christ. Others passively ignore Him. How are their ends equally awful?

4. Jesus tells this parable on Tuesday of Holy Week. In three days, He will take up His cross.

   The Lord's holy Son now wields these words against the teachers of Moses' holy Law and the chief priests of David's holy temple. Why? Does He hurry to damn those plotting His death, or does He still hope to deliver them?

5. You are about to walk with Jesus into Holy Week. See Him take up His cross for you, your sins, your guilt!

    Do you hear the Lord's holy Son wield words of Law against you? He would show you your sins! Does He hurry to damn you? Or did He die in His sure hope to deliver you?

6. Explain the change God's Spirit brings to the lives of God's forgiven people (Ephesians 4:32). What does this change mean to you?

Vision

During This Week

1. Have you lovelessly let go of a friend's sin against you? Can you help him or her turn toward our heavenly Father with heartfelt sorrow and faith? You can echo Jesus, speaking His Law and Gospel with love!
2. Have you lovelessly refused to forgive your enemy's sin against you? If so, have you turned toward our heavenly Father with heartfelt sorrow and faith? Take to heart Jesus' love! And towards your enemy, live Jesus' love!

Closing Worship

Pray together Psalm 103:8–17a. Leader/Participant by whole verse, all together on verse 17a.

The LORD is compassionate and gracious,
    slow to anger, abounding in love.
He will not always accuse,
    nor will He harbor His anger forever;
He does not treat us as our sins deserve
    or repay us according to our iniquities.
For as high as the heavens are above the earth,
    so great is His love for those who fear Him;
as far as the east is from the west,
    so far has He removed our transgressions from us.
As a father has compassion on his children,
    so the LORD has compassion on those who fear Him;
for He knows how we are formed,
    He remembers that we are dust.
As for man, his days are like grass,
    he flourishes like a flower of the field;
the wind blows over it and it is gone,
    and its place remembers it no more.
But from everlasting to everlasting
    the LORD's love is with those who fear Him,
    and His righteousness with their children's children.

Scripture Lessons for Next Sunday

Read Deuteronomy 32:36–39; Philippians 2:5–11; and Luke 22:1–23:56 in preparation for the next session.

Session 6

Palm Sunday
or Sunday of the Passion

Deuteronomy 32:36–39; Philippians 2:5–11; Luke 22:1–23:56

Isa 50-4-9ⁿ *MK*

Focus

Theme: *The Day in the Life of Jesus*

Law/Gospel Focus

The days in the life of humankind are dark and dreary as a result of a sinful, disobedient existence apart from God. But God intervened in our life by placing His Son on the cross as our substitute, and as a result, our days are full of His light and life.

Objectives

By means of the Holy Spirit working through God's Word we will

1. examine the meaning of Christ's substitutionary death on the cross for our sins;
2. believe *the day* of Jesus' death results in new meaning for all the days of our lives;
3. confess with words and lives of service that "Jesus is our Savior."

Opening Worship

Pray together the Introit for Palm Sunday:

Leader: Into Your hands I commit my spirit;
Participants: Redeem me, O Lord, the God of truth.
Leader: In You, O Lord, I have taken refuge;
Participants: Let me never be put to shame; deliver me in Your righteousness.
Leader: Into Your hands I commit my spirit;
Participants: Redeem me, O Lord, the God of truth.
Leader: Let Your face shine on Your servant;
Participants: Save me, O Lord, the God of truth.

41

Introduction

1. List the five most important days in your life. Rank these from
most to least important.

    day of Marriage - anniversary
    " Childbirth
    Christmas
    Easter

2. What makes these days so important to you?

3. Now think about your relationship to God. List the most important days in your faith-relationship with your Lord. Were some of
these days included in the most important days of your life? Why
or why not?

Inform

Read the following summaries of the Scripture lesson for the Sunday of the Passion.

Deuteronomy 32:36–39—The Lord reveals again that He will
judge His people and have compassion on them. The Lord identifies
Himself as the sovereign who has mercy on those who repent of their
sin and trust solely in Him.

Philippians 2:5–11—Jesus' humiliation and God's exaltation of
Him deal with the reality of who our Lord is. His successful work on
our behalf means that ultimately the whole world, on the last day, will
confess Jesus as Lord.

Luke 22:1–23:56—The passion events of Holy Week begin to
unfold in the Gospel lesson. The story of Judas' plot, the Last Supper,
the time of prayer on the Mount of Olives, Peter's betrayal, the trials
before religious and secular leaders, Jesus' death on the cross, and His
burial are all part of *the day* of Jesus' death.

1. How does the Lord show Himself as the true and sovereign God (Deuteronomy 32:36–37)?

2. In the Old Testament reading God heals, brings to life, and delivers His people. According to the following passages, in what ways has He done this?
Psalm 34:18 *saves crushed spirits*

Ephesians 2:8–9
Saved by grace – a gift of God.
Not works

Titus 3:5

3. What Christlike attitudes does Paul urge us to have in Philippians 2:7–8?
Not saved by works
- according to his mercy
- rebirth + renewal by Holy Spirit

4. How might we rightly respond to the fact that God exalted Jesus to the highest place (Philippians 2:10–11)?
We should bow down before him
& confess that he is Lord

5. Why are each of the following events important and/or meaningful to you?
The Last Supper (Luke 22:7–20)
New covenant with God

Jesus in the Garden (Luke 22:39–46)

He offered himself up to ~~Jesus~~ God (handwritten)

Jesus' Trial (Luke 22:54–23:25)

took Him to high priest house exchange murderer for Jesus (handwritten)

The Crucifixion (Luke 23:26–49)

He saved others — Can he not save himself? certainly this more innocent (handwritten)

The Burial (Luke 23:50–56)

Joseph of Arimathea asked for his body — wrapped them in cloth + layed them in the tomb. (handwritten)

Connect

Day after day slides past us as time marches on in our lives. We live for those moments of importance to us.

1. Some days are more important for us than others. Describe how important *the Passion Day* in the life of Jesus was to your life by relating it to the message of these passages.

Isaiah 53:4

He bore our sins (handwritten)

1 Corinthians 15:3

He died for our sins (handwritten)

Galatians 1:4

gave himself — our sins

Hebrews 9:28

Christ offered himself for us + will come again to save us

Revelation 5:9

We are worthy to be saved — God ransomed us

2. The day of Jesus' death brought a radical change in our relationship to God. Paul explains this change when he says "every knee shall bow and every tongue confess."
   a. Because of *the final day* in the life of Jesus, how might you daily bow your knee to Jesus?

   b. How might you confess Jesus is Lord at home? at work? to your friends?

3. *The day* of Jesus' death is the most significant moment in history for us, and yet it happened two thousand years ago. It was at our Baptism that we joined in this event. Read Romans 6:1–4. Why might you say, "Because of my Baptism every day is an important day for me"?

He renews us every day.

45

Vision

During This Week

1. Each day this week write at least one thing that makes the day important to you. Spend a few moments thanking the Lord in prayer for all that He has accomplished for you.
2. Call a friend or relative and share with them the message of Christ and His Lordship in your life.

Closing Worship

Sing together "Take My Life, O Lord, Renew" (*LW* 404; *TLH* 400).

Scripture Lessons for Maundy Thursday

Read Jeremiah 31:31–34; Hebrews 10:15–39; and Luke 22:7–20 in preparation for the next session.

Session 7

Maundy Thursday

Jeremiah 31:31–34; Hebrews 10:15–39; Luke 22:7–20

Focus

Theme: *The Best Meal You Ever Had*

Law/Gospel Focus

Because of sin people are either spiritually dead already (nonbelievers) or spiritually malnourished and in danger of dying eternally from spiritual starvation. God in His grace and mercy recognized our hopeless plight and provided His only Son as a sacrifice for our sins. God continues to nourish us spiritually through the Lord's Supper, providing us forgiveness of sins and eternal life.

Objectives

By means of the Holy Spirit working through God's Word we will
1. thank God for His gifts of forgiveness, life, and salvation provided in His meal;
2. rejoice in the knowledge that God, in Christ Jesus, established a new covenant with each believer through His meal;
3. be strengthened and encouraged for Christian living by frequent participation in Christ's meal.

Opening Worship

Pray together the litany (Psalm 51: 1–3, 12):

Leader: Have mercy on me, O God, according to Your unfailing love;

Participants: According to Your great compassion blot out my transgressions.

Leader: Wash away all my iniquity

Participants: and cleanse me from my sin.

Introduction

"This is the best meal I ever had."

1. Tell about a meal that you would describe as "the best meal I ever had."

2. List the reason you consider it "the best meal I ever had."

3. Do you think you will ever eat another meal that you might describe as "the best meal I ever had"? Why?

Inform

Read the following summaries of the Scripture lesson for Maundy Thursday.

Jeremiah 31:31–34—God promises a new covenant written on the hearts of people. It will enable them to know Him in a personal way. The new covenant is a promise to forgive sin and remember our iniquity no more.

Hebrews 10:15–39—Through the Holy Spirit we realize that the new covenant enables us to draw close to God through our High Priest, Jesus Christ. We are encouraged to live for God and forsake our sinful ways. Our new life will involve standing firm and persevering for Christ.

Luke 22:7–20—The new covenant for humankind was established when Christ gave Himself for our sins and rose again. He seals the new relationship by establishing His Supper of bread and wine in, with, and under which are His body and blood poured out for the forgiveness of our sins.

1. The word *covenant* appears in connection with God's relationship to people. What are God's covenant promises in these passages? Genesis 9:8–13

   Genesis 12:1–3

2. With Jesus Christ came the promised new covenant spoken of in the Old Testament lesson. What promises does God make in the New Covenant described in Hebrews 10:15–18?

3. According to the Epistle lesson what are the results of living under God's new covenant? Hebrews 10:23

   Hebrews 10:24

   Hebrews 10:25

   Hebrews 10:35

Hebrews 10:39

4. According to the Epistle lesson what are the results of living apart from the new covenant?
Hebrews 10:26

Hebrews 10:27

Hebrews 10:29

Hebrews 10:31

5. Without Christ as our great High Priest we would be hopelessly lost to our sins and sinning. Jesus gives us His testimony and then empowers us to keep His covenant when we participate in the Lord's Supper. What else does He offer us in the Lord's Supper (Luke 22:19–2; 1 Corinthians 11:23–26)?

6. Much discussion has occurred over the Lord's Supper. Luther talks about the blessings received from the meal. Read Luther's explanation from the Small Catechism. Underline the blessings Jesus provides to you and to all believers in His Holy Supper.
   "These words, 'Given and shed for you for the forgiveness of sins,' show us that in the Sacrament forgiveness of sins, life, and salvation are given us through these words. For where there is forgiveness of sins, there is also life and salvation."

Connect

Our continued physical existence depends on receiving regular nourishment. There is no difference in our spiritual life. For believers, the nourishment of Word and Sacrament are essential for the growth and strengthening of faith. God's benefits are given in the Holy Meal to all who have faith in the words "given and shed for you."

Read each situation below and relate it to the benefits of the best meal you will ever have.

1. Mary has not been in church since her high school years. She is beginning to feel as if God doesn't care about her. Often she finds herself involved in sinful activities even though she knows they are wrong. Mary attends church one Sunday and decides to partake of the Lord's Supper after she had spoken with her pastor. What benefits did the meal provide her?

2. Sue and Jeff have attended church regularly for their entire marriage. Together they have taken Communion frequently. They have had ups and downs in their marriage but they always seem to forgive one another and forget those things that have come between them. What benefits have they received from their participation in our Lord's Meal?

3. Andy just recently returned to live with his parents. Occasionally, on Christmas and Easter, he would attend church with them. In the last five months, however, he suddenly began to attend more often. He also began to celebrate the Lord's Supper regularly. What benefits did he receive for his faith and life?

The best meal you can ever have to sustain your spiritual life is the body and blood of Christ in, with, and under the bread and wine. In this Holy Meal God strengthens you to overcome your sin and defeat Satan's temptations. In the meal, God comes with His promise that death is not the end, but only the beginning of the new life that He offers to all who believe.

Vision

During This Week

1. Write a prayer in which you thank God for the benefits He has given you in the Lord's Supper, the best meal you will ever have.
2. Write a letter to a friend or relative explaining the joy of knowing that your sins are forgiven and that life and salvation are yours.
3. Joyfully receive the bread and wine in certain confidence that in so doing you participate in the body and blood of Christ and thereby proclaim His death and its benefits for you.

Closing Worship

Pray:

Leader: Oh, give thanks unto the Lord, for He is good.

Participants: And His mercy endures forever.

Leader: As often as you eat this bread and drink this cup,

Participants: You do show the Lord's death till He comes.

All: We give thanks to You, Almighty God, that You refresh us through the Holy Meal; and we ask You to strengthen our faith in You and our love for one another; through Jesus Christ. Amen.

Scripture Lessons for Good Friday

Read Isaiah 52:13–53:12 [Hosea 6:1–6]; Hebrews 4:14–16; 5:7–9; John 18:1–19:42 [John 19:17–30] in preparation for the next session.

Session 8

Good Friday

Isaiah 52:13–53:12 [Hosea 6:1–6]; Hebrews 4:14–16; 5:7–9;
John 18:1–19:42 [John 19:17–30]

Focus

Theme: *The Worst Suffering, the Best Result*

Law/Gospel Focus

Sinners justly deserve a painful and eternal separation from God. God re-established a relationship with people through His Son's death on the cross. He enabled them, through faith, to receive His free gift of forgiveness of sins and eternal life.

Objectives:

By the power of the Holy Spirit working through God's Word we will
1. recognize that Jesus suffered and died as a result of our sin;
2. acknowledge that God freed us from the bondage of evil by means of the cross;
3. thank God for sending His Son to purchase us back from sin and win for us the privilege to become His own dear children.

Opening Worship

Read responsively the verses below (Hebrews 9:12b, 15a; Psalm 111:9a; Isaiah 53:4).

Leader: Christ entered the Most Holy Place once for all
Participants: by His own blood, having obtained eternal
              redemption.
Leader: He is the mediator of a new covenant,
Participants: that those who are called may receive the
              promised eternal inheritance.
Leader: He provided redemption for His people;

Introduction

"We'll send this to the lab for testing, to determine whether it's malignant," the doctor said after removing the small growth from Jose's back. Jose, eager to receive the results of the test, asked, "When will you have the results?" The doctor said, "I'll call you in about a week."

The next days that followed were unbearable for Jose. He couldn't eat or sleep. He was short tempered at home and easily distracted at work. Each day Jose suffered from the anxiety of not knowing. Finally, at the end of the week, the doctor called, "The growth was benign." Jose had suffered, but the result of the test was great.

1. Share a time when you or a family member suffered like Jose.

2. How were the results of the test influenced by the suffering Jose inflicted upon himself?

3. How did the suffering Jesus experienced on the cross have a great result for you?

Inform

Read the following summaries of the Scripture lessons for Good Friday.

Isaiah 52:13–53:12—The innocent Savior, Jesus Christ, suffered and died to atone for our sins. Jesus was despised. Jesus was rejected. Jesus was oppressed. Jesus was afflicted. Jesus carried our infirmities. Jesus bore our sin. All because we, like sheep, had gone astray. Innocently, Jesus suffered the punishment for our sins.

[Hosea 6:1–6]—Only God could bring new life to a disobedient and spiritually dead people. His coming is as sure as the sun rising and the spring rains. God desires that people acknowledge Him and not simply go through the motions of sacrifice.

Hebrews 4:14–16; 5:7–9—Our great High Priest Jesus was like us in every way, except He was sinless. Believers are encouraged to look to Him, to follow His example, and to obey Him.

John 18:1–19:42 [John 19:17–30]—The culmination of our Lord's life is His journey to the cross. The tragic events of those final hours in His life are conveyed, beginning with His arrest and ending with His burial.

1. The central point of the tragic story of the Suffering Servant is found in Isaiah 53:6. Why did Jesus die according to this passage?

2. How does Isaiah 53:12 describe Jesus' death on the cross?

3. The promise our Lord gave goes beyond the cross. How does Hosea 6:2–3 look beyond?

4. What words in Hebrew 4:14–16 describe the activity of Jesus as our High Priest?

5. What do we receive from God? (See Hebrews 4:16.) Why is this important?

6. How does Hebrews 5:7–9 demonstrate the worst suffering and the best result?

7. How does Jesus show He is in control of what will happen to Him? John 18:4–9

   John 18:10–11

   John 18:27; John 13:38

   John 18:36

   John 19:11

8. When Jesus said in John 19:30, "It is finished," what did He mean?

Connect

The morning was every bit as normal as any other for Tom. Then it happened. As he crossed the street he saw the truck coming and knew the vehicle could not avoid hitting the little girl. In a flash and without hesitation he pushed her to safety. Tom lost his life that morning but saved the life of the little child.

1. Compare the suffering and result from this story to the suffering of Jesus and its results.

2. How are the words of suffering found in the Old Testament reading from Isaiah related to your sin?

3. In what ways is innocent suffering the worst kind of suffering?

4. How can we call the day in which our Savior experienced the worst suffering "Good Friday"?

Vision

During This Week

1. Pray that God strengthens your spiritual relationship with Him as you hear the story of the worst suffering, which brought the best result.
2. Choose one of your "pet" sins and ask God for strength in overcoming it.

Closing Worship

Sing or say together "The Agnus Dei" (*LW*, p. 151).

Scripture Lessons for Next Sunday

Read, in preparation for the next session, Exodus 15:1–11; 1 Corinthians 15:1–11; Luke 24:1–11.

Session 9

The Resurrection of Our Lord

Exodus 15:1–11; 1 Corinthians 15:1–11; Luke 24:1–11

Focus

Theme: *He Won the Victory and So Did We*

Law/Gospel Focus

Since the Fall, all people have suffered the consequences of sin, been captive to death, and lived at the tyrannical hand of Satan. Thanks be to God that Christ has gained for us victory over sin, death, and Satan and has empowered us to celebrate His peace and joy in our lives.

Objectives

By the power of the Holy Spirit working through God's Word we will

1. rejoice and thank God for Christ's victory on our behalf;
2. celebrate the life of peace and joy that comes to us through our relationship to Jesus Christ;
3. see the events of life from the perspective of Christ's victory on Easter morning.

Opening Worship

Pray together:

Leader: "Alleluia. Christ has risen, as He said."
Participants: "He has risen from the dead. Alleluia."
Leader: "I will sing to the Lord,"
Participants: "For He is highly exalted."
Leader: "The Lord is my strength and my song;"
Participants: "He is my God, and I will praise Him."
All: "Alleluia. Christ has risen, as He said.
                     He has risen from the dead. Alleluia."

Introduction

Where is the victory celebration for you? In our world today it is easy to focus on our own trials and tribulations. Life is full of problems: bills to pay, broken relationships to mend, and even personal gloom. Where is the victory for you today?

Sue struggled for ten years to earn her college degree. First there were children and then there was the need for a part-time job to supplement the family income. Finally, the day came and she graduated third in her class of three hundred. Months turned to years and still she could not find a job that related to the skills she had acquired in college. Where is the victory for Sue?

Max worked at the auto plant for twenty years. One day the manager came over to him and said that the factory would shut down in three weeks. Max would be one of those who would be out of work. Where is the victory for Max?

1. Share a time in your life when you asked, "Where is the victory for me?"

2. How did God use this trial in your life to bring about "victory for you today"? How is He still at work bringing you "victories"?

Here is the good news! Because Christ has risen from the grave, we also shall live. In Him we are more than conquerors, whether we face life or death, happiness or persecution. Yes, in Him, we can celebrate the Easter victory in all situations. His victory is ours, too!

Inform

Look at the following summaries of the Scripture lessons for Easter Sunday.

Exodus 15:1–11—Moses and the Israelites sang a song of victory after crossing the Red Sea. They joyfully acknowledged that the mighty God had brought about the destruction of their foe and saved them. Their praise rose to the heavens as they proclaimed the works and wonders of the Lord.

1 Corinthians 15:1–11—Paul shares with his readers the proof that indeed Christ has risen from the grave. The evidence of the resurrection is overwhelming—so many saw and believed. The victorious message of God's grace for all people, given even to Paul, the persecutor, is the heart of the Gospel.

Luke 24:1–11—What seemed to be a disastrous defeat on Friday turned into a joyful victory on Sunday. The women came and found an empty tomb. They shared Christ's victory with the disciples.

God has provided the Good News for our victory celebration. Whether it is at the Red Sea, a personal encounter on a road, or in the shadow of a tomb, we see the grace of God. He gave us this victory at our Baptism when we died with Christ and were buried with Him, only to rise again.

1. In the Old Testament lesson, what words are used to describe God as one who had given victory over the army of Pharaoh? (See Exodus 15:1–3, 6.)

2. What did the Old Testament people do to recognize and affirm God as the one who provided the victory? (See Exodus 15:1–2.)

3. According to the Epistle lesson, Paul preached the Gospel of salvation. What was his message? (See 1 Corinthians 15:3–4 and Ephesians 2:8–9.)

4. Why does Paul refer to himself as one "abnormally born"? (See 1 Corinthians 15:8–11.)

5. Compare and contrast the actions of the women in the Gospel reading before and after their arrival at the tomb.

Connect

1. Easter is a day of victory in your life because Christ won the battle over sin, death, and the power of the devil for you. Discuss the various ways you might celebrate the victory of the resurrection today.
   ___ praise God each day by reading His Word
   ___ look to Christ in times of trials
   ___ share the Gospel with others
   ___ attend Bible study
   ___ daily thank the Lord
   ___ other _____
   ___ other _____

2. At times you may share the reason for your joy in life with others. Perhaps they are like the disciples in the Gospel reading, "they did not believe" (Luke 24:11). How might you continue to share your victory?

3. Easter means victory for us! In your own words summarize how the passages describe that victory.
   1 Peter 2:24

   2 Timothy 1:10

   1 Corinthians 15:55–57

1 John 3:8

4. Easter's meaning can elude even believers at times. When economic stress enters a household, a natural disaster occurs, or illness takes one by surprise—we may live in defeat and forget the victory won for us. Martin Luther wrote in "A Mighty Fortress," *And take they our life, Goods, fame, child, and wife, Though these all be gone, Our victory has been won.* In what situations might these words help Christians today? How might the words help you?

Vision

During This Week

1. Spend a few minutes each day thinking about the personal victory the living Lord has won for you over sin, death, and the devil.
2. Focus on a person in your life who seems to walk in defeat rather than victory. Share with that person your thoughts on why you can celebrate.
3. Write a letter to a friend that expresses your joy over the love of God in Christ Jesus, our risen Lord who won for you victory over sin, death, and the power of the devil.

Closing Worship

Sing or pray together "Christ Jesus Lay in Death's Strong Bands" (*LW* 123). Or pray responsively.)

Leader: Sing to the Lord and bless His name, proclaim His salvation from day to day.
Participants: Give to the Lord all glory and strength, give Him the honor due His name.
All: Alleluia! Alleluia!

Leader: Now is Christ risen from the dead and become the firstfruits of them that sleep.

Participants: Give to the Lord all glory and strength, give Him the honor due His name.

All: Alleluia! Alleluia!

Scripture Lessons for Next Sunday

Read Acts 5:12, 17–32; Revelation 1:4–18; and John 20:19–31 in preparation for the next session.

Session 10

Second Sunday of Easter

Acts 5:12, 17–32; Revelation 1:4–18; John 20:19–31

Focus

Theme: *Surprise, Surprise, Surprise*

Law/Gospel Focus

We who are both believing saints and doubting sinners are guilty of Christ's death. We deserved the tree upon which He hung for us. Yet, on our behalf and for us, the loving and risen Jesus overcame sin, death, and the devil in order that we might be saved.

Objectives

By the power of the Holy Spirit working through God's Word we can

1. identify ways God continues to provide us with His forgivness, gracious surprises, and peace amidst our fears;
2. confess the Lord as the source for all good and perfect gifts in our lives;
3. meditate on the faith that God has given us to calm our fears and doubts.

Opening Worship

Pray together (from Psalm 105:1–4, 8):

Leader: Give thanks to the LORD, call on His name;
Participants: Make known among the nations what He has done.
Leader: Sing to Him, sing praise to Him;
Participants: Tell of all His wonderful acts.
Leader: Look to the LORD and His strength;
Participants: Seek His face always.
Leader: He remembers His covenant forever,
Participants: The Word He commanded, for a thousand generations.

Introduction

Often people hear or say, "Life is full of surprises." This response to a situation often implies that an unexpected situation has occurred.

1. What recent events or situations have given you or someone you know the opportunity to say, "Life is full of surprises"?

In a sense, our Lord is full of surprises for us. Instead of being confined to a tomb after dying on a cross, He rose on the third day to the surprise of the disciples. Instead of receiving the condemnation we deserve for our sin, He graciously gives us a great undeserved surprise—His unexpected forgiveness. Instead of hating us because of our sinful self-centeredness, in Baptism God chooses to love us as His very own children.

2. How is God continuing to surprise you in your life?

Inform

Look at the following summaries of the Scripture lessons for the Second Sunday of Easter.

Acts 5:12, 17–32—The cost of discipleship was great. The religious leaders were jealous and vindictive, placing the disciples in jail because of their witness to the living Lord Jesus Christ. But no bars could hold back their message or thwart their mission. God provided a means of escape and Peter declared, "We must obey God rather than men!" (Acts 5:29).

Revelation 1:4–18—John greets the seven churches in Asia Minor and confesses Jesus as the Lord of the church.

John 20:19–31—Jesus surprises His disciples by His resurrection appearances. The first surprise occurs on Easter evening when Thomas is absent. Jesus gives His disciples a greeting of peace, a commission, and the Spirit. A week later Jesus returns and surprises Thomas. Jesus shows Thomas that faith does not rely on physical appearance.

1. What surprises do you find in the first lesson (Acts 5:12, 17, 19)?

2. How is the statement made by Peter in Acts 5:29 a surprise?

3. What does "Alpha and Omega" (Revelation 1:8) mean?

4. Through the Spirit, John peeked into heaven and viewed the Living One. What surprises did he see in Revelation 1:12–16?

5. In the Gospel reading, Thomas doubted and then believed. Describe how this change occurred. (Compare John 20:24–25 with John 20:27–29.)

6. Today we find the surprises of God in Word and Sacrament. In what way does John 20:29 refer to them?

7. Each of the readings has three common elements. Fear is followed by God's surprising intervention that melts fear into peace. Identify the three elements in each lesson.

Scripture Reading	Fear	Jesus' Surprising Intervention	Peace
Acts 5:12, 17–32			
Revelation 1:4–18			
John 20:19–31			

═══ **Connect** ═══

The Lord continues to grant us His blessings of forgiveness, life, and salvation as a result of our Baptism. These gifts come to us as surprises because we confess we are truly unworthy of them. God's surprising intervention and activity in our life come to us today through simple means—water, bread, wine, and His Word. Even in our fear, God's gracious surprises give us peace.

1. What surprises does God give you according to these passages?
   Ephesians 2:8–9

   Titus 3:5

   Romans 15:13

   Matthew 26:27–28

2 Corinthians 5:17

2. Are there times when you have felt like fearful and doubting Thomas? How has God surprised you at these times?

3. What do the three lessons say about your fears? God's surprising intervention? your peace?

4. How has God's surprising activity in your life given you peace? (See Romans 5:1–5.)

Vision

During This Week

1. Meditate on the meaning of John 20:31 as you think about living a life full of God's surprises.
2. Read Romans 5:1 each day and pray to the Lord for His peace in your life.
3. Write about a surprise God has given you.

Closing Worship

Sing or pray together stanzas one and eight of "O Sons and Daughters of the King" (*LW* 130).

Scripture Lessons for Next Sunday

Read Acts 9:1–20; Revelation 5:11–14; and John 21:1–14 in preparation for the next session.

Session 11

Third Sunday of Easter

Acts 9:1–20; Revelation 5:11–14; John 21:1–14 19

Focus

Theme: *Once Was Blind but Now I See*

Law/Gospel Focus

The evil in our lives continues to blind us into believing that serving God involves only what we desire to do. God has brought us from sinful rags to saintly service through Jesus who purchased us from sin, death, and Satan's power.

Objectives

By the power of the Holy Spirit working through God's Word we will

1. acknowledge that sin blinds people to God's desires for their lives;
2. praise God for our gift of spiritual sight made possible by His Son's death and resurrection;
3. compare the Christian's sight and the unbeliever's blindness and relate the differences to life's real meaning.

Opening Worship

Pray together (Psalm 30:1–5):
Leader: "I will exalt You, O Lord,"
Participants: "For You lifted me out of the depths and did not let my enemies gloat over me."
Leader: "O Lord my God, I called to You for help"
Participants: "And You healed me."
Leader: "O Lord, You brought me up from the grave,"
Participants: "You spared me from going down into the pit."
Leader: "Sing to the Lord, you saints of His;"
Participants: "Praise His holy name."

Pray for Jim Daherty – cancer
Kathy Severson sister in law – Jackie Swanson
cancer spread.

71

Sing or pray together "This is the feast" (*LW* p. 161)

> This is the feast of victory for our God.
> Alleluia, alleluia, alleluia.
>
> Worthy is Christ, the Lamb who was slain,
> whose blood set us free to be people of God.
> This is the feast of victory for our God.
> Alleluia, alleluia, alleluia.
>
> Power, riches, wisdom, and strength,
> And honor, blessing, and glory are His.
> This is the feast of victory for our God.
> Alleluia, alleluia, alleluia.
>
> Sing with all the people of God,
> and join in the hymn of all creation:
> Blessing, honor, glory, and might be to God and the Lamb
>   forever. Amen.
> This is the feast of victory for our God.
> Alleluia, alleluia, alleluia.
>
> For the Lamb who was slain has begun His reign.
> Alleluia.
> This is the feast of victory for our God.
> Alleluia, alleluia, alleluia.

(Text: From *Lutheran Book of Worship*, Copyright © 1978.
By permission of Concordia Publishing House.)

Introduction

Close your eyes and move around in a confined area to experience the feeling of physical blindness.

There is not only physical, but also spiritual blindness. In the case of the latter, which afflicts all people, we are unable to see the things of God and we lack the faith to see the risen Christ. By God's grace He opens our eyes through the working of the Holy Spirit in Word and Sacrament.

1. What is the cause of spiritual blindness? (See Romans 5:12, 19; 8:7.)

2. In what ways does this blindness, caused by sin, manifest itself in
   our lives today (Galatians 5:19)? *NT 270*

   idolatry Sorcery - fermentation - anger. flurry. impurity
   strife envy drunkenness etc

3. What miracle has occurred to open our spiritual eyes (Colossians
   1:13–14; 2 Corinthians 5:19; John 3:5–6)? *NT 252 -253   NT 128*

   he rescued us thru his Son -
   We aim to please God.

══════ Inform ══════

Look at the following summaries of the Scripture lessons for the
Third Sunday of Easter.

173 Acts 9:1–20—Only a miracle could change the life of the Christian
hunter Saul into the Christian missionary Paul. On the road to Dam-
ascus, the apostle is confronted by the Lord Jesus who asked, "Saul,
Saul, why do you persecute Me?" (Acts 9:4). God restores Paul's sight
and empowers him to proclaim Jesus as the crucified and living Son
of God.

370 Revelation 5:11–14—Only Christ the Lamb is worthy of our worship because He has won the victory and has taken His place on the
throne in heaven.

156 John 21:1–14—Seven of the disciples decided to go fishing and
when they returned they found Jesus. The risen Christ prepared
breakfast for His disciples to eat with them on the shore of the Sea of
Galilee.

1. In the first lesson, a fundamental change occurs in Paul between
   Acts 9:1 and Acts 9:20. What caused Paul to see Jesus as the cru-
   173 cified and risen Son of God?

   Struck by light from
   heaven.

2. God called upon Ananias to visit Saul. Why was this such a difficult task for Ananias?

   He knew what Paul had done to Christians

3. John was given the sights and sounds of heaven. The sight was spectacular! What key words did he hear and what did they imply about the Lamb (Revelation 5:12–13)?

   310

   every creature on earth

4. How did Peter finally come to recognize the risen Jesus in John 21:5–7?

   158

   by what he said

5. The disciples who accompanied Peter fishing recognized the Savior. What clues did they have? Compare Luke 5:4–7 with John 21:6. How was Jesus different in the latter reading? (See John 21:14.)

Connect

In our Baptism the Lord gave us spiritual sight. He provides us with a new view of life. Compare the sight Jesus gave us to the sight the boy received in the following story:

The day finally came for the doctor to remove the bandages. The child, who had been born blind, now had his moment of sight. When the bandages were removed, the patient saw the faces of his parents and siblings. He stood in silent wonder until he heard his mother's familiar voice calling him, "Matthew, can you see?" As he rushed into her arms he said, "O Momma, is this heaven?"

1. How did your life change when you received, by God's grace, spiritual sight?

2. How do you demonstrate in your life the freedom from blindness Jesus provided to you?

3. How do others know that you "once were blind but now see"?

4. The world is a harvest field for witnessing to the Lamb of God who takes away the sin of the world. Death, Satan, and evil no longer terrorize us for we have fixed our sight on Him who has conquered all. How might you share this sight with someone who is spiritually blind?

5. Read Hebrews 12:2–3 and think about the new sight you have received. In what ways might you continue to fix your eyes upon the one who gave you sight?

Vision

During This Week

1. Rejoice in a prayer of thanksgiving for the sight that God granted in Baptism.

2. Seek an opportunity to witness to a person who is spiritually blind. Talk about the sight that only the risen Jesus can give.

Closing Worship

Leader: The Lord is risen from the grave. Alleluia!
Participants: Who hung for us upon the tree. Alleluia!
Leader: Then were the disciples glad. Alleluia!
Participants: When they saw the Lord. Alleluia!
Leader: This is the day the Lord has made. Alleluia!
Participants: We will rejoice and be glad in it. Alleluia!
Leader: The Lord is risen indeed. Alleluia!
All: And has appeared to us. Alleluia!

Scripture Lessons for Next Sunday

Read Acts 13:15–16a, 26–33; Revelation 7:9–17; and John 10:22–30 in preparation for the next session.

Session 12

Fourth Sunday of Easter

Acts 13:15–16a, 26–33; Revelation 7:9–17; John 10:22–30

16: 9–15

Psalm 67

Focus

Theme: *The Lamb Is the Shepherd*

Law/Gospel Focus

Sometimes evil appears to be winning in our lives, and God seems distant and silent to us. But the Lamb whose blood was shed to free us from sin, remains our ever-present Shepherd who comforts and guides us through life.

Objectives

By the power of the Holy Spirit working through God's Word we will
1. recognize the Lamb of God as God's sacrifice for our sins and the sins of the whole world;
2. acknowledge the Lamb as also the Shepherd who is eager to guide us each moment of our lives;
3. rejoice as we serve the Shepherd.

Opening Worship

Pray together from John 10:14 and Psalm 23:
Leader: "I am the Good Shepherd;"
Participants: "I know My sheep and My sheep know Me."
Leader: "The LORD is my shepherd,"
Participants: "I shall not be in want."
Leader: "He restores my soul,"
Participants: "He guides me in paths of righteousness for His name's sake."
Leader: "Surely goodness and love will follow me all the days of my life,"
Participants: "and I will dwell in the house of the LORD forever."

Introduction

We commonly hear the phrase "A picture is worth a thousand words." List some scriptural pictures of Jesus.

Among the many scriptural pictures of Jesus are the Good Shepherd and the Lamb. Check those activities of the Good Shepherd that seem most important to you personally.

- ☐ Guides
- ☐ Cares
- ☐ Loves
- ☐ Rescues
- ☐ Restores
- ☐ Directs
- ☐ Helps

Give an example from your life of how Jesus has acted as your Good Shepherd.

The irony of the Good Shepherd picture is that He is also pictured as the Lamb of God. How does the picture of Jesus as the Lamb of God describe His action on your behalf?

Inform

Look at the following summaries of the Scripture lessons for the Fourth Sunday of Easter.

Acts 13:15–16a, 26–33—Paul preaches to the assembled members of the synagogue at Antioch of Pisidia on his first missionary journey. In his message, Paul proclaims that God's ancient promises were fulfilled in Jesus Christ. This Jesus is the Risen One written about in Psalm 2, "You are my Son; today I have become your Father" (Acts 13:33).

Revelation 7:9–17—John has a vision about heaven. He describes it as an inclusive place—a great multitude from every nation, tribe, people, and language stand before the throne. Among the residents are those who have come out of the great tribulation and are there because of the Lamb. The focus is on the Lamb of God and the Shepherd, to whom belongs all power, glory, and might.

John 10:22–30—He who is the Lamb is also the Shepherd. Jesus reveals that He is the Christ who is one with the Father. The Shepherd's sheep hear Him, know Him, and follow Him. He provides them with eternal life.

1. Summarize the work of the Lamb as found in each passage.
   Isaiah 53:4–5

   John 10:17–18

   John 1:29

   1 John 1:7

   1 John 2:2

2. Martin Luther once said, "I would not give up one moment of heaven for all the joy and riches of the world, even if they lasted thousands and thousands of years!" He seems to echo Revelation 7:10, 12. How is Luther's claim reinforced by these verses?

3. How are those in heaven described in Revelation 7:15–17?

4. How does Revelation 7:17 impact the pictures of Jesus as Lamb and as Shepherd?

5. How do Jesus' words in John 10:27–29 reassure you?

6. Reread John 10:22–30. List what the Shepherd does and how His sheep respond.
Shepherd

Sheep

Connect

"Violent crime is on the increase." Which of us would dispute that statement? Evil appears to be winning and many Christians are becoming fearful of the future. But the Good Shepherd is still in control, for He has all power, glory, and might. He still controls your life.

"In summary," writes Luther in his explanation to the Seventh Petition of the Lord's Prayer, "[we pray] that our Father in heaven would rescue us from every evil of body and soul, possessions and reputation, ..." What a comforting activity our Shepherd is engaged in on our behalf!

1. How does God's action, described in Psalm 121:7–8, bring comfort to you?

2. What will the Shepherd do in your life when fear and distress occur? (See 2 Thessalonians 3:3.)

3. How do the following "pictures" of the Shepherd bring further comfort to your life?
   John 6:35

   John 7:37

   John 9:5

   John 11:25–26

   John 15:5

4. The Good Shepherd provides for His sheep. Christ also promises us all that we need to support this body and life. What do sheep need spiritually? Check each one that currently applies to you and explain why.
   ☐ Forgiveness of sins
   ☐ Protection from temptation
   ☐ Words of comfort in distress
   ☐ Renewal amid all of life's stresses
   ☐ Peace in knowing He is in control
   ☐ Guidance in Christian living
   ☐ Understanding life's events
   ☐ Assurance of salvation
   ☐ Eternal life

Vision

During This Week

1. Spend a moment each day thanking the Good Shepherd for all that He provides to you, especially for your spiritual life.
2. Tell the story of the Lamb and the Shepherd to a friend, or to a family member.
3. Write a letter to a friend who needs to hear about the care and guidance given by the Good Shepherd.

Closing Worship

Sing or pray together "At the Lamb's High Feast We Sing" (*LW* 126).

Scripture Lessons for Next Sunday

Read Acts 13:44–52; Revelation 21:1–5; and John 13:31–35 in preparation for the next session.

Session 13

Fifth Sunday of Easter

Acts 13:44–52; Revelation 21:1–5; John 13:31–35

Focus

Theme: *What's New about Love?*

Law/Gospel Focus

We no longer want to live life full of sinful retribution and hatred. Christ's death and resurrection have freed us from the bondage to evil. Through His Spirit He gives us faith, providing us with a new life focused on love for one another.

Objectives

By the power of the Holy Spirit working through God's Word we will
1. acknowledge that although because of sin, people's love is often motivated by selfishness rather than selflessness—God loves us with a pure, genuine love;
2. affirm Jesus' sacrificial love as our motivation to love others;
3. seek God's strength to overcome sin and to demonstrate Christian love.

Opening Worship

Pray together (Psalm 145:1–2, 8):
Leader: "I will exalt You, my God the King;"
Participants: "I will praise Your name for ever and ever."
Leader: "Every day I will praise You"
Participants: "And extol Your name forever and ever."
Leader: "The LORD is gracious and compassionate,
Participants: "Slow to anger and rich in love."

Introduction

Sin has distorted and destroyed God's idea of love. Many people today ask: "What is love?" Compare the lyrics to the Beatles' song, "All you need is love …" to Jesus' words "love one another." So … What is love?

1. Describe *love* as portrayed in each of the following examples.
   a. John and David were the best of friends. It seemed that people would frequently find them together wherever they were. They would do anything for one another.

   b. Does she really love me? Lonnie wondered to himself. He was plotting exactly the right way and the right moment to kiss his girlfriend in order to show his love.

   c. Sue was driving home from work one day, and for no apparent reason stopped and befriended a homeless person. She purchased a bag of groceries and then took her to the local homeless shelter. She was late getting home that night.

Love is not easy to define. Is it? Often the definition involves our motives, which are tainted by sin. Since we are both saints and sinners, those motives can certainly become confused.

2. Name some positive and some negative motives for "love."
   Positive

Negative

Inform

Look at the following summaries of the Scripture lessons for the Fifth Sunday of Easter.

Acts 13:44–52—Paul, the missionary sent by God to proclaim the Good News, preached first to the Jews and then to the Gentiles in Pisidian Antioch. God's chosen people rejected the message, while the Gentiles received it and were led by the Spirit to believe. The "Word of the Lord spread" (Acts 13:49).

Revelation 21:1–5—The final chapter of history is seen in an apocalyptic vision. The present fallen world comes to an end and God establishes a new heaven and earth. Evil, death, sorrow, and pain will come to an end. Even now the old is in the process of being changed into the new by the power of God, "I am making everything new!" (Revelation 21:5).

John 13:31–35—This event occurred during the final week in the life of our Lord. Jesus was in the upper room with the disciples. Judas had just fled after having been exposed as a traitor. Jesus again announced to the disciples that He must die and that by His death He would demonstrate His love for them. He commended to His followers a new commandment, "As I have loved you, so you must love one another" (John 13:34).

1. How do the Jewish residents of Pisidian Antioch demonstrate the exact opposite of love toward Paul and Barnabas?

2. At times God's love in Jesus Christ is rejected by people. Why did Paul react the way he did by moving on to another city? (See Acts 13:48–52.)

3. God's love is new for us each day. What does He promise to those He loves? (See Revelation 21:4.)

4. Why are people totally incapable of the love God desires that they have for others? (See Genesis 8:21.)

5. When Jesus makes us new creations in Baptism, He also empowers us to love one another. What examples of love does Jesus provide in the passages below?
   1 John 3:16

   Titus 2:14

6. Through His love for us, God motivates us to love. Love manifests itself in our external actions. What does Jesus say is the result of our love actions? (See John 13:35.)

7. So, what is new about love? Disciples of Christ are called to demonstrate the type of love exemplified by the Savior as He gave His life for us. How "new" that love is from the self-centered love we find in our world. His love replaces the world's vindictiveness. His love rejects hatred. His sacrificial love replaces selfishness. Read 1 Corinthians 13:4–7 and summarize God's description of love, motivated by His love for us in Jesus.

Connect

Demonstrations of Christian love in our lives flow from the boundless love God has given to each of us in the death and resurrection of His Son.

1. Look at each case below and write how we might demonstrate God's love to each individual. Remember God in Christ forgives all repentant sinners—no sin is too great for Jesus to forgive.

   a. A person in your church convicted of child abuse.

   b. An adult child who steals his or her older parent's life savings.

   c. Individuals involved in a family argument that occurs during Thanksgiving dinner.

2. What motive do you as a Christian have for loving others? How does your motive differ from an unbeliever's motive?

3. Showing love at times means doing the same thing Paul did in Acts 13:51: "So they shook the dust from their feet ..." and left that place. This might be referred to as "tough love." How might exercising "tough love" eventually cause a person to turn to Jesus. If time permits read 1 Corinthians 5:1–5. What "tough love" have you experienced? What "tough love" have you shared?

Vision

During This Week

Identify a person this week to whom you can show Christian love. First, ask for God's help in demonstrating your love for that person. Then write as many ways as you can think of to act in love toward the person. Choose one or two suggestions and begin to demonstrate that love.

Closing Worship

Sing or pray together stanzas one and four of "Dear Christians, One and All" (*LW* 353).

Scripture Lessons for Next Sunday

Read Acts 14:8–18; Revelation 21:10–14, 22–23; and John 14:23–29 in preparation for the next session.

Session 14

Sixth Sunday of Easter

Acts 14:8–18; Revelation 21:10–14, 22–23; John 14:23–29

16:9-15   or 67

Focus

Theme: *Departures and Arrivals*

Law/Gospel Focus

In the darkness of sin, people search for or create gods of their own as they reject the true God. Nevertheless, God calls us to faith in Jesus as the Holy Spirit works through His Word to bring us into a loving relationship with Him, and to comfort us when we face life's trials and tribulations.

Objectives

By the power of the Holy Spirit working through God's Word we will

1. examine the life of a Christian as thanking, praising, serving, and obeying God;
2. acknowledge the comfort given by the Spirit in the departures and arrivals of life;
3. rejoice that the Spirit comes to us in Word and in Sacrament to strengthen our faith and to assure us of God's love.

Opening Worship

Pray together (Psalm 66:1, 2, 8, 9, 20):

Leader: "Shout with joy to God, all the earth!"
Participants: "Sing the glory of His name;
  make His praise glorious!"
Leader: "Praise our God, O peoples,"
Participants: "Let the sound of His praise be heard;"
Leader: "He has preserved our lives"
Participants: "And kept our feet from slipping."
Leader: "Praise be to God,"
Participants: "Who has not rejected my prayer
  or withheld His love from me!"

Introduction

I moved my possessions into my assigned dormitory room at college with the help of my parents, and the reality of our imminent separation began to overcome me. As the car began to pull away I wanted to run after it. In my heart I called, "Stop! Stop! Don't leave me here!" ...

Vacation was coming. First it was but ten days away, then nine, until finally the day to go home arrived. I anticipated my time at home with excitement and joy. When I arrived home I threw open the door and shouted, "I am home for Thanksgiving vacation!"

Departures and arrivals are sometimes difficult and sometimes joyous.

In the Gospel lesson appointed for today, Jesus prepared His disciples for both His departure and for the arrival of the Holy Spirit.

1. How do you prepare for departures, such as a child leaving home for college, or for family members leaving after an Easter visit?

   By accepting they have their lives & we have ours & we have to do whats best for all.

2. Describe the arrival of a loved one to your home. Was it a joyous occasion for you? Why or why not?

   anxious awaiting & joy
   Not always - because expectations aren't always the same

3. Can you think of a time when the departure of someone you loved was good for you and for him/her, even though it might have been painful?

   finding out Jerry was dead & Pete having such a hard time accepting it.

Inform

Look at the following summaries of the Scripture lessons for the Sixth Sunday of Easter.

Acts 14:8–18—When the unbelievers of Lystra see the miracle of healing the man crippled from birth, they shout, "The gods have come down to us in human form!" (Acts 14:11). Paul and Barnabas insist they are only humans who have been given a message from the living God.

Revelation 21:10–14, 22–23—The Spirit provides a glimpse of heaven to John. He sees the Holy City, the new, shining Jerusalem with surrounding walls and gates. In contrast to Palestinian Jerusalem, there is no earthly temple in the city of God. Instead, God Almighty and the Lamb are the temple.

John 14:23–29—Jesus speaks about His departure from earth and promises the coming of the Holy Spirit. Love forms the basis of the relationship between the Father and the Son, and of God's relationship with us. Jesus' love for us compels us to obey Christ's teachings.

1. Paul wrote that sinful people exchanged the "truth of God for a lie, and worshiped and served created things rather then the Creator" (Romans 1:25). How does this apply to the first lesson? (See Acts 14:11–13.)

2. Paul and Barnabas brought the Gospel message with them to Lystra. They must have felt like departing after being misunderstood by the people. Instead, what did Paul and Barnabas do? (See Acts 14:14–15.)

3. In the Spirit, John arrived to see the Holy City of God. In Revelation 21:11–14 he identifies a great, high wall; twelve gates with each having an angel and the names of the twelve tribes of Israel; and twelve foundations with the twelve apostles' names. Discuss the meaning of the high wall? the twelve gates? the names of the twelve tribes? the twelve foundations?

4. In John's vision, who is the source of light? Who serves as the temple in heaven? (See Revelation 21:22–23).

91

1480+

5. In John 14, Jesus tells about His departure—He will soon be crucified and will rise on the third day. Describe what Jesus shares with His disciples.

   a. How is love related to obedience (John 14:23–24)?

   those who love Me keep my word
   Father will love them

   you will obey

   b. Who is the object of our love (John 14:23)?

   us + God.

   c. What is the object of obedience (John 14:23–24)?

   If you dont love you wont keep
   God word.

   d. What will the Counselor do (John 14:26)? *(Holy Spirit)*

   we will be taught everything +
   be reminded what God has taught
   us.

   e. From where does peace come (John 14:27)?

   from. God / Holy Spirit , oneness with God

   f. For what reasons does Jesus share these things (John 14:28–30)?

   Because he was going away to be
   with God & God's love was greater

   I give you peace

Connect

The disciples did not understand the meaning of our Lord's departure and His promise of the Spirit's arrival. They considered only what they wanted to hear rather than understanding the comforting words of the about-to-depart Jesus. Sometimes we do the same.

1. How have you, or someone you know, responded to the following events?

    _____ The loss of a loved one *deep sadness but also joy that they are with God*

    _____ Separation from a family member *– a longing to make the separation go away.*

    _____ Loss of a job *– deep loss of usefulness*

2. As Jesus departed, He promised to send the Comforter to His disciples. How might the following passages provide a basis for comfort when events like the ones mentioned in question 1 happen?
Nahum 1:7 *cf 12:c*

    God is good – He will protect us

   v⁺ 2:9 Romans 8:38–39

    Nothing can separate us from God's love.

    Psalm 23

    took me in your arms loved me even tho I was not worthy

Vision

During This Week

1. In prayer, thank God this week for all His goodness throughout your life in the past and in the present. Ask Him for His continued blessings in the future.

2. Send a card to a friend who is enduring a sadness due to a departure. Emphasize God's comfort in times of tribulation.
3. Rejoice with a family member who is celebrating a joyous event in his/her life.

Closing Worship

Sing or pray together "Our Father, Who from Heaven Above" (*LW* 430).

Scripture Lessons for the Ascension of Our Lord

Ascension Day—Read Acts 1:1–11; Ephesians 1:16–23; and Luke 24:44–53 in preparation for the next session.

Session 15

The Ascension of Our Lord

Acts 1:1–11; Ephesians 1:16–23; Luke 24:44–53

Focus

Theme: *I Told You So!*

Law/Gospel Focus

Since Adam and Eve fell into sin, the hearts and minds of people have been closed to the things of God and unable to know the one true God. Through the Gospel, God opens our eyes and empowers us to see and hear the Good News of the crucified, resurrected, and ascended Christ so that we might witness His love for all people through our words and deeds.

Objectives

By the power of the Holy Spirit working through God's Word we will

1. acknowledge Jesus as the crucified, risen, and ascended Lord and Savior who has fulfilled all righteousness on our behalf;
2. confess Jesus as the one who sits at the right hand of God our Father for the benefit of His people;
3. joyfully praise God from whom all blessings flow.

Opening Worship

Pray together (Psalm 47:5):

Leader: "God has ascended amid shouts of joy,"
Participants: "The LORD amid the sounding of trumpets."
All: Grant, we pray, almighty God, that even as we
                   believe Your only-begotten Son, our Lord Jesus
                   Christ, to have ascended into heaven, so we may
                   also in heart and mind ascend and continually
                   dwell there with Him; who lives and reigns with
                   You and the Holy Spirit, one God, now and
                   forever. Amen.

Introduction

Over and over his father had told him that he must always drive the speed limit. He tried! He really tried! But there was always a little voice inside that told him, "No, not you. You can go as fast as you want and nothing will happen." Now the lights in his rear view mirror had a different message: They were irritating, those alternating red and blue flashing lights. He must pull over and stop. First came the bright light in his face and then the voice through the window. His heart was pounding. He knew he was caught! He was guilty of driving fifteen miles over the speed limit. Now he would have to go home and hear his father's voice say, "I told you so!"

1. Describe times when someone said to you, or you said to someone, "I told you so!"

   ashamed - I should have known better
   resent the teller

2. How do the words "I told you so!" affect the receiver?

   resentment - put down

   Jesus told His disciples that He would be going away, and then promised to send them His Spirit. They would be witnesses before the whole world to what had happened. During those days and through the coming years they would need to remember that Jesus had "told them so."

3. How does Jesus continue to tell us about ourselves and our lives?

   by the things that happen -
   we know - we just need to be reminded

Inform

Look at the following summaries of the Scripture lessons for Ascension Day.

Acts 1:1–11—The disciples saw the risen Christ over a period of forty days until the Ascension. During this time, Jesus taught them about the kingdom of God and commanded them to wait in Jerusalem for the Holy Spirit to come. He told them of their future mission, "You will be My witnesses in Jerusalem, and in all Judea and Samaria, and to the ends of the earth" (Acts 1:8). They watched Jesus ascend into heaven and received the promise that He would come again.

Ephesians 1:16–23—Paul gives thanks for the people and prays that the Spirit of wisdom and revelation be given to them. He focuses on the source of the Christian life—the crucified, risen, and ascended Lord. Jesus was appointed as head over everything for the sake of the church.

Luke 24:44–53—Jesus teaches the meaning of Scripture and relates it to His life. He commissions His disciples as witnesses and promises them the Spirit to assist them in their task. After Jesus ascends into heaven, the disciples worship Him and praise God constantly in the temple.

Indicate with a check mark those statements which are true about Christ's ascension into heaven. Then read each passage.

☑ 1. Jesus gave many proofs that He was alive before He ascended into heaven (Acts 1:3).

☐ 2. The disciples were told to wait in Jerusalem for a gift (Acts 1:4–5).

☑ 3. The disciples were told by Jesus they were to be witnesses (Acts 1:8).

☑ 4. Jesus will come back in the same way the disciples saw Him ascend (Acts 1:11).

☑ 5. The Spirit helps us to know Jesus better (Ephesians 1:17–19).

☑ 6. God enlightens those who believe in Him about the hope and riches of being God's children (Ephesians 1:18).

☑ 7. Jesus is seated at God's right hand (Ephesians 1:20–21).

☑ 8. Christ is the Head over everything for the sake of the Church (Ephesians 1:22).

☑ 9. Jesus told His followers everything in Scripture about Him was to be fulfilled (Luke 24:44).

☑ 10. Jesus told His disciples about Himself and how they fit into His plan (Luke 24:46–49).

☑ 11. The disciples responded to Jesus' ascension with joy (Luke 24:52).

☑ 12. After Jesus ascended into heaven, the disciples worshiped and praised God (Luke 24:52, 53).

Connect

"I told you so!" characterizes the last days of Jesus as He prepared the disciples for His ascension. He has also prepared us for daily discipleship. Jesus suffered and died on the cross to purchase us back from sin. By His resurrection from the dead He proclaimed victory for us over sin, death, and the power of the devil. The Holy Spirit, working through God's Word and sacraments, continues to strengthen our faith, empowering us to live our lives as His disciples. Read the passages and relate their message to your life:

Psalm 34:22

Let your steadfast love be upon us even as we hope in you.

Psalm 118:8

It is better to take refuge in the Lord than in mortals

Proverbs 3:5

trust in Lord - do not rely on your own insight

John 16:24

ask & you will receive

1 Thessalonians 5:18

give thanks in all circumstances

When we say "I told you so!" we usually do so in order to demonstrate our correct insights into a situation. How are God's "I told you so's" different? *all promises - I will do for you*

Perhaps you remember a comforting "I told you so" passage (like your confirmation verse) from God's word. Share why it provides you comfort in your life.

Vision

During This Week

1. Write your "I told you so!" verse on a note card and include it in a letter to a friend who needs the assurance of God's promise.
2. Thank God each day for the forgiveness He grants to you as a result of the person and work of Jesus Christ. Ask Him for strength to remain steadfast in His Word.
3. Call a close friend and share with him/her the message of God's "I told you so!"

Closing Worship

Sing or pray together "Up through Endless Ranks of Angels" (*LW* 152).

Scripture Lessons for Next Sunday

Read Acts 16:6–10; Revelation 22:12–17, 20; and John 17:20–26 in preparation for the next session.

Ryon - Bogue .
mary wintermute
wayne Greer - strict Treatment
Floyd - Heart L gall bladder)

Session 16

Seventh Sunday of Easter

Acts 16:6–10; Revelation 22:12–17, 20; John 17:20–26

Focus

Theme: *Behind Closed Doors*

Law/Gospel Focus

Sin closed the door for people to know God, destroying the perfect relationship between God and people that existed in the Garden of Eden before the Fall. Christ Jesus restored the broken relationship and opened the door for eternal life with Him. The Holy Spirit, working through God's Word, guides, comforts, and directs us through this life to the door into eternity, Jesus Christ.

Objectives

By the power of the Holy Spirit working through God's Word we will
1. recognize that the Lord leads, guides, and directs His people through doors of opportunity, while closing other doors;
2. rejoice that God continually blesses and sustains us in order to bring about His gracious plan for us;
3. pray for the unity of God's church that it may be one in Christ by being one in confession.

Opening Worship

Pray together (Romans 6:9; John 14:18):
Leader: "Alleluia. Alleluia. Since Christ was raised from the dead,"
Participants: "He cannot die again;"
Leader: "Death no longer has mastery over Him.
Participants: "Alleluia."
Leader: "I will not leave you as orphans;"
Participants: "I will come to you."
All: "Alleluia. Alleluia."

Introduction

There was once a very unpopular but powerful businessman who died. Two of his former colleagues saw the obituary notice and decided to go to the funeral. When they arrived, they found the church so packed they could not find a seat. Said one, "Look at all these people. How do you explain it?" Said the other, "Give people what they want and they will come out from behind closed doors."

It seems ironic that closed doors should be discussed during the season when we celebrate the open tomb of our Lord.

1. What events typically take place behind closed doors in your life or the lives of others?

2. Sometimes we close a door to hide something, and at other times because we fear something. When have you or someone you know closed a door for one of these reasons? If you feel comfortable doing so, describe the situation.

Inform

Look at the following summaries of the Scripture lessons for the Seventh Sunday of Easter.

Acts 16:6–10—Asia Minor and Bithynia were closed doors for the Gospel preaching of Paul. But God opened the doors to Macedonia. In a vision, God called Paul to proclaim the Gospel. God says "no" as well as "yes." After one door is closed the Spirit opens another door for the spreading of the Gospel.

Revelation 22:12–17, 20—The coming of the Lord is imminent for His people. He will come again to judge each person according to his deeds. He will declare those who have believed in Christ, "Not guilty," and invite them into heaven. Those who remain outside the kingdom are the ones who continue to reject saving faith in Jesus as the only way to heaven. "Yes," Christ promises, "I am coming soon" (Revelation 22:20).

John 17:20–26—The reading is a part of Jesus' High Priestly Prayer offered at the Last Supper. Knowing He will soon ascend to the Father, Jesus prays for His disciples and for future generations. He focuses on the unity of those who believe. Christian harmony demonstrates the love of God in Christ to the world. Jesus also prays that His followers will be with Him in heaven where they will see the glory the Father has given Him. His final prayer is that His followers will continue to know and love God.

1. What doors did the Spirit close for the Apostle Paul? (see Acts 16:6, 7.) What door was opened? (See Acts 16:8.)

2. What was the purpose of Paul's vision? (See Acts 16:10.)

3. None of us is worthy, but Jesus opens the door to heaven for us. Who is eligible to enter? (See Revelation 22:14.)

4. The door of heaven is closed to some. Who are they? (See Revelation 22:14.)

5. What is the invitation God gives to all people? (See Revelation 22:17.)

6. Why are the words of Jesus in Revelation 22:12 and 20 important?

7. For what does Jesus pray in John 17:21?

8. Throughout the Gospel reading what does Jesus tell us about His relationship with the Father?

Connect

The Lord is so gracious to us. While we were sinners—while we desired to exist and live with the doors of our hearts closed to Him and His will—He opened wide the doors of our hearts through Baptism and freely gave us forgiveness of sins. We are now His; the door has been opened. In His love for us, Jesus continues to guide and direct our lives.

1. In the past, what "life" door has God closed for you or someone you know? What benefit did God bring you through this?

2. In the past, what door in your life has God unexpectedly opened? What benefit did God bring you through this?

3. Connect the Lord's action in your life to the passages below.
   Psalm 23:2

   Psalm 48:14

Psalm 73:24

Isaiah 30:21

John 10:11

4. How might you apply Jesus' prayer for unity to opening a "door" among the fellowship of believers in your congregation?

5. As Jesus hangs on the cross and is about to enter the door of death, He says, "Father, into Your hands I commit My spirit" (Luke 23:46). Death is our final door, but where does it lead? Read 1 Corinthians 15:55–58. Apply the questions below to your life.
   a. Death has no victory over you because ... (v.55)

   b. You can thank God for victory because ... (v. 57)

   c. You can stand firm and immovable because ... (v. 58)

   d. You can give yourself to the Lord's work because ... (v. 58)

Vision

During This Week
1. Pray Psalm 143:10 each day.
2. Watch for God's activity of opening and closing doors in your life.

Thank God in prayer for His guidance and direction.
3. Reach out to a friend who feels the sadness and sorrow of having a door closed to him/her. Comfort the person with God's promise.

Closing Worship

Sing or pray together "Christ Is the World's Redeemer" (*LW* 271).

Scripture Lessons for Next Sunday

Read Genesis 11:1–9; Acts 2:37–47; and John 15:26–27; 16:4b–11 in preparation for the next session.

Session 17

The Festival of Pentecost

Genesis 11:1–9; Acts 2:37–47; John 15:26–27;16:4b–11

(handwritten margin notes: "— Celebration Session", "hype", "Call", "gather", "enlighten", "sanctify")

Focus

Theme: *Gathering to Scatter*

Law/Gospel Focus

As surely as God punishes those who reject Him and seek to build their own self-serving community, He promises to send the Holy Spirit to establish, build, and strengthen His community through the Word and through the sacraments.

Objectives

By the power of the Holy Spirit working through God's Word we will

1. recognize God's call to worship centered around the Word and the sacraments;
2. demonstrate confidence in our lives of daily discipleship because of the Holy Spirit, our Comforter and Guide;
3. recognize the challenges of being in the world, and yet not of the world.

Opening Worship

Pray together this adaptation of "Come, Holy Ghost, God and Lord," *LW* 154:

Leader: "Alleluia. Alleluia. Come Holy Spirit, God and Lord,"

Participants: "Fill the hearts of Your faithful people, and kindle in them the fire of Your love."

Leader: "Alleluia. Alleluia. Come, holy Light, guide divine,"

Participants: "Teach us to know our God aright."

Leader: "Alleluia. Alleluia. Come, holy Fire, comfort true."

Participants: "Grant us the will Your work to do and in Your service to abide."

All: "Alleluia. Alleluia. Come, Holy Spirit."

Introduction

Every four years the athletes of the world meet to compete in the games of the summer and winter Olympics. At each Olympiad the lighting of the Olympic Flame marks the beginning of the games. The flame is ignited by a torch that runners have carried from the Olympic Valley in Greece to the host city, and it burns throughout the games as a symbol of the Olympic spirit.

Our Lord promised to send His Spirit to the Church, His community of faithful followers. After waiting for days the Spirit came on Pentecost to ignite the disciples' faith. As the lighting of the Olympic Flame marks the beginning of the Summer or winter Games, so the coming of the Holy Spirit at Pentecost marks the beginning of the Christian church. His coming is more than mere symbolism, however, for He "calls, gathers, enlightens, and sanctifies the whole Christian church on earth, and keeps it with Jesus Christ in the one true faith."

1. When we received the Holy Spirit in Baptism, what did God begin?

2. As the Holy Spirit works through the Word and through the sacraments, what does God continue to do?

═══════ Inform ═══════

Look at the following summaries of the Scripture lessons for Pentecost.

Genesis 11:1–9—By the confusion of language, God prevents the building of Babel and scatters the people. The fear of being scattered had caused these men to build a city and a tower. They wanted to make a name for themselves above all other names by building a tower that would reach heaven. But God confused their language so that they would not understand each other, and the building project soon ceased. People then scattered across the face of the earth.

Acts 2:37–47—The disciples are gathered in Jerusalem on Pentecost when there is a sound like a mighty wind and tongues of fire come upon them. They receive the Holy Spirit promised by Jesus before He ascended into heaven. Peter preaches repentance and forgiveness—the result: three thousand are added to the church. Believers devoted themselves to spiritual growth through the Word and through the sacraments. As a community of faith they engaged in the activities of prayer and fellowship, as they continually met in the temple courts and in their homes.

John 15:26–27; John 16:4b–11—Jesus promises to send the Counselor, the Holy Spirit. The Spirit will testify of Jesus and will be with the disciples when Jesus leaves. It is the Spirit who convicts the world of sin and condemns the evil in the world. Through God's Word the Spirit also creates and sustains saving faith in Jesus.

1. Why did God scatter the builders of the Tower of Babel? (See Genesis 11:5–6.)

2. How did God respond to the sin of those at Babel? (See Genesis 11:8–9.)

3. What happened when the hearers of Peter's sermon realized their sin? (See Acts 2:36–38.)

4. God gathers His people in His church around the Word and the sacrament. Review Acts 2:42–47 and name the variety of activities which continued in the Church after Peter's Pentecost sermon.

5. For what reason does God scatter those whom He has gathered? What directions to the scattered Church are found in the following passages:
   Matthew 5:14–16

   Matthew 16:24

   Galatians 5:13

   Galatians 5:22–23

   Ephesians 5:18–20

6. When and how did our Lord keep His promise of sending a Counselor? Compare John 15:26 and John 16:7 with Acts 2:1–4.

7. Luther referred to the Holy Spirit in his explanation to the Third Article of the Apostle's Creed, "… He calls, gathers, enlightens, and sanctifies …" How does the Spirit work in your life?

Connect

The three readings speak about the Holy Spirit's work in our lives through the means of grace. How do the following Scripture references apply to your life?

In the Text	My Life Connection
1. "Repent and be baptized ... for the forgiveness of sins." (Acts 2:38)	
2. "They devoted them-selves to the apostles' teaching and to fellow-ship, to the breaking of bread and to prayer." (Acts 2:42)	
3. "Every day they continuedto meet together in the templecourts ..." (Acts 2:46)	
4. "And you also must testify..." (John 15:27)	
5. "I will send Him [the Counselor] to you ..." (John 16:7)	

As we gather to worship, the Holy Spirit works through God's Word and through the sacraments. He kindles in us faith for the daily struggle with sin, death, and Satan. As the congregation scatters, the Holy Spirit empowers the people for discipleship in the home, at school, and in the workplace.

Vision

During This Week

1. Telephone a different person in the congregation each day and encourage him/her by sharing how God has worked, and is working in your life.
2. Reflect on how God gathered you and now scatters you into the world for sharing His love with unbelievers.
3. Reach out to one other person this week with the message of God's love for them in Jesus Christ.

Closing Worship

Sing or pray together "Come, Holy Ghost, God and Lord" (*LW* 154).

Scripture Lessons for Next Sunday

Read Proverbs 8:22–31; Romans 5:1–5; and John 16:12–15 in preparation for the next session.